PRAISE FOR *STRANGER NO MORE*

"This heroic and granular plight of a refugee will turn your heart towards the broken and displaced. Yes, you will wince at the grit and reality of a life torn by tragedy—and yet you will also come near to a life redeemed by a God who reveals His strength in weakness. You simply will never be able to look at the refugee crisis thru the lens of superficial statistics anymore. And yet you will also celebrate how an intentional, purposeful Savior chooses to intervene against human brutality. An inspiration."

—Benjamin K. Homan, president of Langham Partnership

"Every single person is on a journey to know Jesus, even though we may not often know it or see it. Annahita Parsan shares an amazing, inspiring, and gripping story about her journey to a faithful Savior. You won't be able to believe all that she endures and you certainly won't be able to put the book down once you start. This story gives us a fresh perspective on the refugee crisis we face today."

—E. Andrew Mayo, president and CEO of the
Medical Benevolence Foundation

"Tremendous to read *Stranger No More*. I pray that many more Muslims will fasten their gaze on Jesus, as Annahita Parsan has done. They will discover that God is love. Thank God for non-Western theologians, such as Annahita. There is more to discover about God's love and glory, and Christians who read the Bible through Middle Eastern eyes have a unique contribution to make. Don't stop now, Annahita. I am sure there is a second God-glorifying book inside you that will bless us as this one has."

—Bob Blincoe, PhD, president of Frontiers USA
and author of *Ethnic Realities and the Church*

STRANGER
NO MORE

STRANGER NO MORE

A Muslim Refugee's Story of Harrowing Escape,
Miraculous Rescue, and the Quiet Call of Jesus

ANNAHITA PARSAN

WITH CRAIG BORLASE

NELSON
BOOKS

An Imprint of Thomas Nelson

Published in Nashville, Tennessee, by Nelson Books, an imprint of Thomas Nelson. Nelson Books and Thomas Nelson are registered trademarks of HarperCollins Christian Publishing, Inc.

Published in association with the literary agency D.C. Jacobson & Associates, LLC, an Author Management Company, www.dcjacobson.com.

Thomas Nelson titles may be purchased in bulk for educational, business, fundraising, or sales promotional use. For information, please e-mail SpecialMarkets@ThomasNelson.com.

Scripture quotations are taken from the Holy Bible, New International Version®, NIV®. Copyright © 1973, 1978, 1984, 2011 by Biblica, Inc.® Used by permission of Zondervan. All rights reserved worldwide. www.Zondervan.com. The "NIV" and "New International Version" are trademarks registered in the United States Patent and Trademark Office by Biblica, Inc.®

Any Internet addresses, phone numbers, or company or product information printed in this book are offered as a resource and are not intended in any way to be or to imply an endorsement by Thomas Nelson, nor does Thomas Nelson vouch for the existence, content, or services of these sites, phone numbers, companies, or products beyond the life of this book.

ISBN 978-0-7180-9572-7 (eBook)
ISBN 978-1-4002-0751-0 (IE)

Library of Congress Cataloging-in-Publication Data

ISBN 978-0-7180-9571-0
Names: Parsan, Annahita, 1962- author. | Borlase, Craig, author.
Title: Stranger no more : a Muslim refugee's story of harrowing escape, miraculous rescue, and the quiet call of Jesus / Annahita Parsan with Craig Borlase.
Description: Nashville : Thomas Nelson, [2017]
Identifiers: LCCN 2017019194 | ISBN 9780718095710
Subjects: LCSH: Parsan, Annahita, 1962- | Christian converts from Islam--Biography.
Classification: LCC BV2626.4.P37 A3 2017 | DDC 248.2/4670092 [B] --dc23 LC record available at https://lccn.loc.gov/2017019194

Printed in the United States of America

17 18 19 20 21   LSC   10 9 8 7 6 5 4 3 2 1

This book is dedicated to my two children, Daniel and Roksana. Their wisdom, encouragement, and understanding have seen me through the darkest times, and gives me hope for the future. I am blessed to have them by my side.

All Glory to God who made this book possible.

CONTENTS

PROLOGUE

ASAD WAS DOING A BAD JOB OF HOLDING in his anger. He stood at the front of the church, his back to the congregation, fists balled and staring at the wall behind me. Between the lack of eye contact and the years-old beard, I guessed he was maybe a little fanatical. But not so much. A true Islamic fundamentalist wouldn't be in a church having a conversation with a woman like this. Unless . . . I glanced down. Thankfully his shirt was way too tight around the middle to be hiding anything dangerous.

"Why are you trying to convert people?" he said.

I told him that I really was not and that I would be happy to talk with him just as soon as the church service was done.

He glowered a little and turned tail.

I was praying for someone when he came back. The air was pretty heavy in the church. God was at work all over the room. And Asad walked right into the thick of it. As soon as he got within a few feet of the front, he fell right down and stayed there for twenty minutes.

He was a little confused when he finally came around. "Where am I?"

"In church."

"What happened?"

"God wanted to talk to you."

And that's when the tears came.

He cried so long that the church was all but empty by the time he stopped. I asked him whether he had any questions.

"No," he said quietly as he got up to leave.

The next week, right at the end of church, Asad was back. Back marching up to the front, back flat out on his back, and back sobbing.

"Do you have any questions, Asad?"

This time he looked right at me. "Will you pray for me?"

The third week was a little different. He had a shopping bag with him.

"Take this," he said. "I don't want them any more."

It was a Qur'an and some other religious books.

"But I want a Bible in return," he added.

———

Do you want to know the thing I love most about Asad's story? It's not so much what happened in the beginning, with God getting his attention in such a powerful, dramatic fashion. It's what came later. It's the way that God showed Asad—as well as his nine-year-old daughter—just how much he loved them both. It's the fact that within a year they were both baptized, and that today, they are continuing to say yes to all that God invites them into.

And I love that it reminds me of my own story too. I was a refugee and a Muslim, just like him. I was lost and wounded. And when at last I said yes to God, he began to transform everything about my life.

PART ONE

ISFAHAN, IRAN

COME," MY GRANDMOTHER SAID, JERKING
me up to my feet. My whole family called her Khanoum, a title
that conveyed the respect and honor she deserved. "We must
hurry," she whispered. I did not delay, following her out of the
mosque the same way that I had followed her in—my eyes locked
down on the ground in reverence. Ever since I was a young child I
had made these little journeys, accompanying Khanoum to pray
at least once a week. Our visits always ended this way, with her
rushing out and me chasing after. As the prayers of a thousand
voices ended and the march of a thousand pairs of feet began,
Khanoum would lead our dance through the crowd of women,
all hooded and caped in black chadors that made them seem, to
me at least, like ravens robbed of flight.

From an early age I had known to link my steps in with hers,
imagining there was a short, invisible string between us. I still
pretended it was there when I was thirteen, but by then I also
allowed myself to look up and around me. As we passed beneath
the ornate walls that stood taller than any tree I had ever seen,
I stared at the vaulted ceilings that shone above. Their blue and
gold tiles always made me feel as though I was at the bottom of an
ocean, that above the roof was some unknown, mysterious world.

"Faster, Annahita," she said, as I fumbled with my shoes

outside. Though I was already as tall as her, it was still a struggle to keep up as Khanoum sped down the alleys that bunched up behind the mosque. *The string is being stretched tighter than usual today*, I thought.

When we reached her house off Farshadi Street, I assumed that Khanoum would relax. Like any Muslim girl, I knew the change that came across a woman as soon as she crossed the threshold into her home. Once the door shut and the chadors were removed we could all lose the act. Laughter would return to our world, as would music and color. But that morning Khanoum did not remove her chador. She did not laugh or joke or impersonate the pompous men who paraded about the mosque. Nor did she twirl around the kitchen, and her feet and eyes did not dance in time as she prepared the black tea, fruit, and cheese.

She just moved in silence. I watched, equally mute, following her to the courtyard outside when our simple meal was ready.

Khanoum's courtyard was one of the finest I knew of. Two pomegranate trees stood guard by the tall metal gate, their branches never seeming to run out of the fruit that hung ripe and red. A pool as big as any bed I had ever seen sat in the middle. It was painted blue inside and out, the better to show off the fish that lived within. Low cushions lined the wall to the old house, dwarfed by the tall windows with peaked arches filled with colored glass. Though the world was alive outside its walls, Khanoum's garden was an oasis, and like the house it accompanied, belonged to a time when the city of Isfahan was home to a tide of wealthy merchants.

I sat next to Khanoum on the cushions and watched the pool.

My glass was half empty by the time she spoke.

"Annahita, do you know how old I was when I married?"

I shrugged.

"I was thirteen years old. It was not my choice, but it was my duty. My husband was also my cousin, and he was twice my age. I knew nothing of what it meant to be the wife and woman that he wanted. I was just a child. He did not treat me well."

The silence returned. I knew it was not my place to break it.

"After four years he left me. He married another woman and moved to Tehran. I was still a child, and younger than you are now, so I went to live with his mother, my aunt. For five years we begged him to return, pleading with him to come back and lift the burden of shame from over me, but he refused. His compromise was to wait until I was eighteen years old and divorce me. A little of the shame left me, but I no longer had the protection of his family, so, once again I had no choice but to marry. On the day that we married, that man, your grandfather, was more than twice my age."

I had heard part of this speech before. I knew that my grandfather was much older than Khanoum, old enough for him to be little more than a vague wisp of memory to me. And I knew that she had been married before. But married at age thirteen, when she was even younger than I was now? That was new.

The information was not the only piece of the puzzle that was new. I had not seen Khanoum in this kind of mood before. I had always known her to be strong, to be the kind of woman who would not drop her speed or miss a step as she passed the mullahs outside the mosque. But this was different. It was as if a part of her was missing.

Two glasses sat between us, one empty, the other untouched. Khanoum reached out her hands and curled them around mine. Her eyes held me just as tight as her fingers.

"Annahita," she said, her voice almost cracking. "I am

worried about you. I am worried that my bad life will repeat for you."

Somehow, I knew she was right.

———

I stood up from the dirt and checked my wounds. My knee was sore, both palms were scratched, and I could taste blood in my mouth from a cut on my lip. *Nothing too bad*, I thought.

"Again!" I shouted. I watched my brother Hussein wrestle the bicycle back upright and wheel it to the end of the alley that opened to the bright sunlight of the main road.

"You want me to go slower this time?"

"No," I shouted back, hands on hips to make it perfectly clear that I was more than a little offended at the question. "Go faster."

Hussein climbed astride our dad's bike and started to push. Within a few yards he had picked up enough speed for him to transfer his feet shakily to the pedals. A little farther along and he had tamed the bike itself, stopped it from wobbling, and was picking up speed as he came straight for me.

My brother was my elder sibling and my very best friend. I had a younger sister, Mariam, and another little brother too, Ali, but when I was old enough to love the taste of adrenaline and young enough to still be allowed to play, it was my older brother Hussein whose company I cherished the most.

Custom dictated that I could not play with the other boys who lived nearby, and many of my cousins were older and lived too far out of the city for me to visit on my own. Yet even if they had shared our house, I doubt I would have wanted to play with them half as much as I wanted to play with Hussein. He was everything I needed. He made me laugh, and he kept life interesting. He taught me how to play soccer, how to ride a bike, and, whenever I was injured, how to make a choice somewhere deep within to ignore whatever pain I was in and keep going.

Not all of the skills he taught me were quite as useful. Like trying to jump onto a bicycle as it sped past. But as his feet blurred and the alley was filled with the sound of rattling metal as he pedaled toward me, I was determined to meet the challenge he had set for me. *I'm not going to end up in the dirt again*, I told myself as Hussein passed me. I timed my sprint to perfection, reached first one then the other hand out to the fat leather saddle, and leapt.

Hussein is three years older than me, so by the time I was thirteen he was more than old enough to drive. Not that our father agreed. According to him, Hussein was not yet ready, and whenever my brother asked for the keys to the family car—an olive-green sedan made right there in Iran—the answer was always no.

Hussein may have been older, and the firstborn male as well, but I had a special place in my father's heart. On the few occasions that I fought with Hussein—which was only ever when his friends came over and I would try to come outside and see them—my father always took my side. So it was only natural that I be the one to ask for the keys whenever we wanted to try our hand at driving. All I had to do was wait until the afternoon when my father started drifting off to sleep on one of the floor cushions in the living room. Then he would not stop to ask why I wanted the car keys or what I intended to do. He'd simply reach into his pocket and hand the bunch over.

Caught between mountains to the west and desert to the east, summers in Isfahan were often brutally hot. The sun was particularly fierce one particular day, with temperatures getting close to 110 degrees, when Hussein and I snuck out with the keys. It suited Hussein and me just fine as we knew the streets would be empty while the city slept through the hottest part of the day. I handed my brother the keys and opened the heavy metal gates at the front of the courtyard.

It took a little practice for Hussein to edge the car carefully down the alleyway and out onto the main road without grinding the gears. My own driving was a little less advanced, mainly because the cushions I relied upon to help me see over the steering wheel made the pedals just a little too far out of reach. But I was determined not to give up, so I dutifully waited my time while Hussein took the first turn at the wheel.

We drove alongside one of the many canals that fed the city of Isfahan in the way we often did, in silent appreciation of the way the dry breeze filled the car and the water reflected back the sunlight like a trail of scattered diamonds.

The shouting only started when Hussein allowed the car to drift too close to the edge of the road and the front wheel slipped off the tarmac. The car pulled sharp to the right, the canal loomed, and, were it not for Hussein's strong right foot on the brakes—and the fact that he never drove very fast in the first place—we would have driven right in. As it was, the car came to a stop with two wheels off the road, stuck in the muddy banks of the canal. After we caught our breaths, we took turns attempting to reverse the car back out onto the road again, but no matter how hard we tried, neither of us could. We had no choice but to wait and survey the damage to the front fender.

Eventually the sun dipped a little, people emerged from their afternoon naps, and some kind strangers came to our rescue. They hauled us out, but there was nothing we could do about the damage to the front of the car. Again we drove in silence, only this time no amount of beauty could have lessened the fear I felt.

I should not have been surprised that Hussein was given a stern lecture about how irresponsible he had been. And I should have known that my father would have looked at me the way he always did—his head to one side, his eyes sparkling, and his arms offered in an easy embrace.

My mother, however, was less pleased. She folded her arms and stared before telling me how I had let her down. My little sister and brother watched from behind her legs. They knew not to interrupt.

In Iran there are two types of women. Some are weak. They accept everything that happens to them, act out of fear, and allow themselves to be ruled by the men. Almost from the moment these women are born they look to their fathers and their brothers for security. Once they marry they place all their trust in their husband, and so spend their entire lives under the thumb of men. My mother was not one of these.

Though my own father and brother were sources of love and security for me, my mother was one of the main reasons why I knew I was never going to grow up weak and timid. My mother belonged to the other type of Iranian woman—the sort that is strong, independent, and courageous. While the weaker women in Iran allow themselves to be dominated by men and religion— much like so many women from the Arab countries to the west of my homeland—my mother saw herself as a Persian woman, the sort who valued education and refused to let a man treat her as property.

Almost a thousand years before my homeland was turned to Islam, Iran was the heart of the Persian Empire. From the snow-capped mountains in the North to the wide sandy plains of the South, ancient rulers like Cyrus and Nebuchadnezzar oversaw a glorious time in our history. Throughout their territories which often stretched as far as Europe and Africa, women were not treated as second-class citizens, nor were they hidden from view. In fact, in ancient Persia women could own property, be economically independent, and travel.

So, like everyone else I knew, my Persian history was far more important to me than stories of Islam. Those tales felt like secondhand memories to me. All I really knew of Mohammed was that he was the reason I kept my eyes down at the ground as I walked through the mosque. All I really knew of God was that he was far, far away.

———

Sitting beside Khanoum in her courtyard, her hands holding mine tight, the empty glass of black tea in front of me, I was confused. I had always thought of Khanoum as being strong like my mother. The two of them would so often be working side by side, Khanoum barely taller than my mother's shoulder. Despite her size, everyone in the house would hang on Khanoum's every word. She could conjure laughter like a master magician and our house was always happiest whenever she was within its walls.

I had grown to see her as the kind of woman who chose never to hide from a battle, never to allow a man to push her too far.

She was strong, and she was fearless. To me she was the woman who parted the crowds, the lady who carried life and laughter wherever she went.

She was also a devoted Muslim. She had little time for the pompous mullahs and clerics, but she loved God—who we called Hodda, not Allah. Khanoum prayed five times a day. They were the only times when her smile and laughter would be absent. I had always thought she was just being a good Muslim, but I was wrong. To my grandmother, prayer was not about the outward appearance. It was a desperate attempt to have God protect the people that she loved. She prayed in fear to an angry God, not out of faith that she would be helped.

I was too young at the time to understand it all fully, but that afternoon, hearing Khanoum worry about my future, that was when I first discovered there might be more danger and pain in life than I had encountered thus far through my childhood pranks. Would my life really follow Khanoum's? Up until that point I would have been happy if it had—happy to end up strong and bright and fearless like her. I had never considered her life to be harsh or her story to be a cautionary tale. But as we sat in silence it was clear that a cloud had descended over her, weighing her down like an immovable chador, robbing her of freedom, joy, and light.

I think that on that day a part of that very same cloud clung to me too.

MY MOTHER EXHALED A CLOUD OF foul-smelling tobacco smoke as the hookah pipe fired into life. She sat with my father, my uncles, and my two brothers at the side of the room, sharing the pipe as they watched the rest of us get to work. The smell and noise of the hookah so repulsed me that I knew I had the better deal than Ali or Hussein, who were coughing hard, looking nauseated, and giving the adults something to laugh about.

I helped clear away the dishes that covered the sheet spread out across the floor. Thirty of my cousins, aunts, and uncles had visited us that afternoon, and we filled our stomachs on lamb kebab cooked on metal knives as long as my arm, tender rice mixed with saffron, and so much Coca-Cola I thought my insides would burst. As the floor cleared and the cloud of smoke around the men grew thicker, it was time for the most important part of the evening.

Iranians dance better than any other people on earth. At least, that was how it appeared to me as the cassette player clicked on and the whole room took to its feet and started moving as one. It was always infectious to see my family dance like this, their arms held wide and high, their hands tracing circles while their bodies melted from one side to the other in time to the beat. But it is always the eyes that are the things to watch in the best dancers. I loved nothing better than to dance among the crowd myself, seeing up close the laughter, the life, and the love that shone out from each face.

Here there were no mullahs or chadors, no strict religious rules, and no need to stare at the floor in mock humility. The air was full of heat and music, laughter and smoke. And when one of my elder cousins emerged from the bathroom, wearing his mother's dress and dancing like a bride on her wedding day, the laughter only got louder.

The cassette played song after song, each one driving the dancers to keep on moving, like a heart sending out fresh blood to tiring muscles. And when the fast songs faded and a ballad finally struck up, the room took the cue as one to break for a while and allow a dozen conversations to strike up at once.

But not me.

I was crouched down by the cassette player, my hands moving over the rough brown fabric that covered the speakers. I was transfixed by the sound coming from them. I could not name the instruments then as I could now, nor did I know that the voice that belonged to one of the most famous singers ever to come from Tehran. But I knew precisely what I was listening to; it was the sound of such pain and sorrow that I feared it would steal my breath.

The man was singing about a poppy flower, but I knew it was about so much more. He sang about the way the poppy is always alone, how it cannot be with others. He described the way his heart and eyes were both red like the flower. His life was short, he said, just like the poppy's. Death would visit them both soon.

It was as if someone had taken me by the hand and walked

me to the mouth of a cave filled with the darkest sorrow of all the world. I was amazed that anyone could feel so strongly and still be alive. The song and the emotions it contained fascinated me. It was like staring into a flame or looking up at the sky as a storm came in over the mountains to the west. It left me transfixed. At times, it held me captive.

———

For several months I listened to that song over and over. Even when I was not crouched by the speakers, trying to hold my breath against the smell that came from my dad's hookah, I could summon it in my head.

The song would often play loudest in my head when I visited Khanoum. Most days after school I would pick my way through the alleys and turn onto Farshadi Street, my mind on the notes of the poppy song. I rarely felt miserable or thought specifically about dying poppies as I walked, but there was something about the deep pain and sorrow, the feeling of being trapped by inevitable fate, that both spoke to me and frightened me. I always looked forward to the moment when I could close Khanoum's door behind me and rip off the chador from my head, breathing deeply with a rush of freedom. My mother had only recently made me start wearing one, but even though I loved her deeply, there was no way that I was going to follow Khanoum's example and wear the sort that fitted tight around my face. And there was no way that it would be black either. Instead I chose one that was full of bright colors, and I wore it far back on my head. Even so, I hated it. I couldn't walk more than ten paces without it getting caught in my bag.

Sitting by the pool, watching the fish as they jumped for

whatever scraps of food I passed them, Khanoum and I would talk. I would tell her about my day, about my friends or my studies, and Khanoum would fuss over me. "You need to eat," she would say, encouraging me to return to the plates of bread, cheese, and fruit and glasses of black tea rich with cardamom, cinnamon, and sugar. "You need to get strong, you need to be healthy." She rarely said more than that, but it was enough to remind me of her warning about the troubles she feared I might face in my life and the God who might or might not intervene. By the time I put my chador back on and said good-bye to Khanoum, I'd be humming the doleful melody as I walked back home.

My mother was a practical woman, and she told me repeatedly that every woman in Iran needs to know how to make money. And so, when I was thirteen, and the hot winds of summer covered Isfahan with desert dust, I spent three months learning how to sew at a summer school a short walk from my home. I quickly picked up the basic skills and was soon able to make simple outfits. I got a thrill from seeing the clothes take shape, and applied myself diligently to every task that was set.

Perhaps, I thought, that was why, in the final week of the course, one of my teachers asked whether I would want to marry her son. I was shy and my words stuck firmly in my throat, so the conversation died then and there. By the time summer school ended, I had nearly forgotten all about it.

The teacher, however, had not. I returned to the summer school the following year, and this time she did not wait until the final days to bring the subject up again.

"Annahita," she said one afternoon as I added some final stitches to a dress while the classroom cleared around me. "I think you are a good girl. My neighbor's son is studying but wants to be married. Would you like to be married?"

"I'm not sure," I said.

Some days later, a friend I was studying with told me that she had heard about the teacher's suggestion. "I know this man, Mohammad, " she said. "He is my husband's brother and a good man. Would you like to see him?"

I didn't *not* want to see him, so I shrugged and squirmed a little and agreed to go to her home the following day. There was no chance of Mohammad and me actually speaking when he visited my friend's house, and there seemed little harm in taking a look.

Iranian culture and custom had set in place some clear rules for how members of the opposite sex should interact. There was no dating, and the concept of boyfriend and girlfriend was unheard of. I knew that I would marry young, but I also knew that whatever choice I eventually made would be a choice for life. Divorce would not be an option.

So I proceeded with caution. When Mohammad sent word through my friend that he would like to marry me, I simply said, "I don't think so" and left it for another year.

When my third summer at the school came around and the teacher once more approached me to ask whether I had given any more thought to her neighbor's son, I knew that my mind had changed.

"Yes," I said, looking up from my work. "I think your son needs to come visit me at my home in Isfahan."

The summer had long gone and the air was getting cold by the time Mohammad's father, mother, brother, and sister-in-law followed my own parents, uncles, aunts, sisters, brothers, and Khanoum out of the room and closed the door behind them. The two of us were left alone, Mohammad looking smart in his beige suit, me feeling so nervous I thought I would never stop shivering.

I had never been in a situation like it. Hussein and Ali were the only boys I had ever been alone in a room with before. I was struggling with the chador I was wearing, trying to keep it in place without making too much fuss. I had picked out a special chador for the meeting, one that was covered with bright flowers, and I wore it far back on my head, the way that made the teachers cross at school. I suppose I didn't want to look like the kind of girl who would be weak and timid.

"Those chadors are bad, aren't they?" he said with a smile. "I don't really like them that much."

I returned his smile and gave up trying to fix the mess of hair and fabric on my head. "No," I said. "I don't either."

We talked a lot after that. Mohammad made me laugh with funny comments that reminded me of the kind of thing that Hussein would say. I found that my nerves were soon a distant memory, and they only returned a little when he told me that he was in the army, currently studying to become a helicopter pilot. "The army does not let soldiers marry until they have served five years," he said. "I have one year left to wait."

I don't think either of us knew what to say after that. We both knew what his visit meant.

Eventually, it was Mohammad who broke the silence. "My mom died when I was ten, my dad married another woman, and I don't have anything that could help our future. I don't have any money, but I know that I will do everything for you." I knew then that he loved me. I was fifteen, but I knew that his love was real and that his respect for me was true.

As was the custom, I was given time to think about Mohammad's proposal. There was no need for pressure and no need to rush. For a month I did not talk about any of it with anyone else. I did not need to, for I had already made up my mind. And when my uncle approached me a month after Mohammad's visit to ask for my answer, I was ready to say yes.

Mohammad's family had already visited our friends and neighbors to ask about our family. Once I had spoken with my uncle, my parents had also traveled to visit their neighbors to find out all they could and confirm their hopes that the rest of Mohammad's family was as honest and upright as I was convinced he was.

Everything was carried out exactly as it was supposed to. My parents agreed the dowry that Mohammad's family would pay in the unlikely event that we divorced or Mohammad died. It was a formality, but Iranians have a high view of marriage, and the formalities mattered. Before the winter came, we were engaged.

I COULD NOT SLEEP. OUTSIDE IN THE street the men had started shouting "Allahu Akbar" again. They had been shouting for a whole week, standing on rooftops and filling the night with their cries about the greatness of God. I wished for the hundredth time that they'd be quiet and let the rest of the city sleep.

Something was different this night. The air smelled strange.

I left my room in search of my parents and found my father standing outside in our courtyard, staring up at the sky.

My father had always been kind and gentle, his smile forming easily on his lips and his laugh falling readily from his lungs. But there had also been times when his laughter and smiles were strangers to him. That night, as I stood beside him and tried to see what he was looking out at, I could feel the change within him.

"What's that smell?" I asked as the foul smell returned stronger than ever.

"The mullahs have gotten people angry," he said. "So the young men are burning cars."

It took a long time for him to speak again, but when he did his voice—though it was barely above a whisper—was full of sorrow.

"These people are no good for our country. They talk about

the Shah being corrupt, but they're fools if they think this man Khomeini will be better. Iran cannot be run from a mosque."

I had seen television reports about Khomeini and knew enough already to understand. It was 1979 and, after two generations of the Shah family ruling Iran, things were changing. Both the Shah and his father had turned our country's eyes toward the West, encouraging education and trade with other countries. Religion had been kept far away from politics, but things were changing. Khomeini was a cleric who had recently returned from exile and had been stirring up dissent among those who were angry at the Shah's wealth and their own poverty.

As a sixteen-year-old counting down the months until she got married, I had no great love for religion or politics. For me, the main problem with Khomeini was the impact his followers had on my sleep, plus the fact that in recent months I had been told by too many of my teachers to exchange my bright chadors for black and wear them so far forward that they covered my hair completely.

Most of the time I did what I was told, until it came time to choose my wedding dress. I was in no mind to compromise. My mother insisted that I wear a traditional white wedding dress, the sort that was pure white and that covered everything but my neck and face. I refused. I had found a white dress that stopped a little short of my ankles with a pattern of red flowers on it. The flowers reminded me of the poppy from the song that I had listened to so much before I met Mohammad. Even though the ballad's aching sadness felt a lifetime away, I still felt inexplicably drawn to the red flowers, as if they and I somehow belonged together.

—

My wedding day finally arrived, and I stood outside my home with my father. When he saw my dress, he just smiled—the same smile he had given me when Hussein and I had returned home with a damaged car and guilty faces.

We were waiting for Mohammad's parents to arrive and ask for permission to take me back to their home. It was an act that would mark the end of my father being responsible for me and the beginning of my life with my new family. We stood in silence for the longest time before my father spoke.

"You are leaving in a white dress," he said. "You must come back in a white dress."

He did not have to say anything more. My choice to marry Mohammad was not one that I could go back on. I was leaving as a bride and would not be accepted back should the marriage end in divorce. I was leaving home for good, and we both knew that the only way I could return would be in a white shroud at my funeral.

My father's words did not leave me troubled or angry. I agreed with him fully. What I was about to undertake was a solemn and special thing. I was not acting on a whim, nor was I planning on giving up when marriage became difficult. I was marrying Mohammad and was prepared to devote the rest of my life to him.

The rest of that day and the one that followed it remain bright in my mind to this day. I remember the warmth of Mohammad's smile when he first saw me and the joy of the dancing that lasted until the sky was alive with stars. There was a second party that started early in the morning, when so many guests arrived to bring us gifts that they piled high on the tables in the courtyard. And I remember the image of the two of us staring back as we read the Qur'an to each other in front of a mirror. "You are looking at the future," said the mullah as we paused and stared. It was a sight that sent warmth through every cell of my body.

We spent our honeymoon in the city of Shiraz, where we ambled among the gardens and laughed quietly whenever we saw the mullahs walking around as if they were on parade. We joined all the other newlyweds having their photographs taken, only, when it came time for me to stand in front of a particular fountain, Mohammad suggested I take my chador off. The freedom and the risk made me feel even more alive.

Life was good with Mohammad. We had just enough money to rent a house together, and I soon fell pregnant. Even though the revolution was gathering pace and threatening to sweep Khomeini into power, I felt as though we were insulated from the rest of the world. Like the baby growing safe within me, we were separate from what was going on outside our home. Or, we were until the revolution finally delivered Iran into the hands of the Islamic leaders.

Overnight Mohammad's job as a helicopter pilot changed. He was now answerable to a mullah, rather than a superior officer, and there were rumors of a possible war with our neighbor Iraq. Like all the soldiers, Mohammad was not happy about any of these changes, but he knew he was powerless to change any of it.

I was not surprised when he came home one afternoon and

told me he was being sent to the western border in preparation for war. "I can't leave you alone," he said. "Perhaps Khanoum should come and stay with you."

I told him that my pregnancy was barely showing and that I could manage fine on my own, but, if it made him feel better, I was happy for Khanoum to come. Secretly, I was relieved at the thought of not being alone. If Khanoum was with me, surely everything would be just fine.

───

Later that night, neither of us could sleep. There were the usual shouts of "Allahu Akbar" from the street outside, but both of us had long since gotten used to those.

"It would be better if we had a boy than a girl," he said, stroking my belly.

I withdrew a little. "What? You prefer boys to girls?"

"No," he said softly. "But when my mom died all the problems that my sisters faced were so much worse than the ones I had to deal with. They could not leave the house. They could not escape and join the army. They became like prisoners."

He paused. "Annahita," he said. "One day I'll die." I wanted to protest and tell him that he was foolish to talk like that, but no words came to my mouth. All I could do was listen as he carried on. "Growing up without a mom is hard. If we were in danger and I had to choose between your life and mine, I would rather it happen to me so that you can care for the child."

The silence between us became heavier with every breath.

───

25

The next day Khanoum arrived and Mohammad left. Two weeks later he was back, and a new pattern of our life together was set. He would be at home for a week, maybe two or three, and then suddenly one day he would deliver the news I hated the most, telling me that the next morning he would be gone again.

The times when he was away became like bitter medicine to me. Every day that passed brought the familiar ache of missing him, as well as the familiar fears about what might have happened to him. But they also brought his return another day closer. All I had to do was last them out, and eventually we were always reunited.

After a handful of these trips, my mind was overtaken with other thoughts. My belly was big and my baby was ready to come out. And when my boy, Daniel, finally arrived in the world and Mohammad drove the three of us home from hospital, I thought my life was just about as perfect as it could ever possibly get.

And for ten days, that's exactly what it was. Perfect.

I woke up to hear Mohammad breathing heavily beside me. Daniel was sound asleep between us, but Mohammad was sitting up in bed, his eyes fixed and wide. He was shaking, like he was cold, but his body was covered in sweat.

"What is it? What's wrong?"

I could tell that my words were taking time to sink in. Gradually he turned to me. "It's nothing," he said. "My dreams." I lost him again for a moment, and the shivering returned.

"I dreamt that I died," he said, looking at me with eyes heavy and red with tears.

We both cried for a long time. I had never seen him like this, and I had never known him to have a bad dream. Even though I knew that his time on the border was often terrifying, it never seemed to affect him when he was at home. I had no idea whatever could have caused this nightmare, and I did not know how to bring him the peace he needed.

We dozed a little after that, cradling our sleeping son between us as the daylight leaked into the room. At some point I heard Mohammad stir, get dressed, and return to the bed to kiss us both good-bye. After eleven months of marriage the smell of his cologne had become familiar enough to make me smile deep down inside. I glimpsed him through blurry eyes and drifted off back to sleep.

It was the last time I ever saw him in our home.

AS SOON AS I HEARD THE DOOR OPEN, I exhaled in relief. Daniel had been crying almost from the moment that Mohammad had left early that same morning. I had tried everything to calm him, but nothing had worked. For most of the first ten days of his life Daniel had slept and fed, but something had changed in him and I couldn't wait for Mohammad to come back and drive us over to my parents' house on the other side of the city.

It wasn't just Daniel's cries that had been bothering me. Mohammad was supposed to be home at 2 p.m., just like always. But 2 p.m. had come and gone, and there was still no sign of him. With no phone and no car for me to drive, all I could do was wait and bounce Daniel up and down as I walked around the house.

I was changing Daniel in the bathroom when I heard the front door open and close. I called out to Mohammad, but the voice that replied was not his.

"Annahita?" said my father. "Where are you?"

I walked out to see him, standing by the door, looking tired.

"I thought you were Mohammad."

"No, he had to go to the border unexpectedly," he said. "So he telephoned and asked me to come and take you to our house."

It didn't make sense, but the thought of going back to my

mother and having her help with Daniel banished any questions from my mind.

My dad picked a long route back home. Instead of taking the freeway he cut down side streets and back alleys. "Why are we going this way?" I asked, too tired to try and hide the frustration in my voice. "The other way is much quicker."

All he said was that the freeway was closed. For the rest of the journey my dad drove in silence while I held Daniel tight on my lap and realized how angry I was at Mohammad for leaving to fight without even coming home to say good-bye.

As soon as we arrived home, my dad disappeared, taking Hussein and Ali with him. That made me angry too. I had been looking forward to sitting with them all at home, playing music and laughing just like we used to. Instead, the house felt like a museum, with my mother and sisters almost totally silent, acting as if they were scared of disturbing Daniel.

I didn't like the way so much had changed in so short a space of time, but I was more bothered by the fact that that Mohammad still didn't call that evening.

——

The next day was the same. My dad and brothers were nowhere to be seen while my mother and sister Mariam tread around the house like mice. Even Khanoum was missing, and as the hours inched by, I became increasingly angry with Mohammad for leaving me in the middle of such a mess.

Things were the same the next day.

And the next.

It was only on the fifth day that something changed. My

uncle walked into the house and sat down next to me. He fussed over Daniel for a while before he spoke.

"Do you know where your husband is?"

I felt so very young, as if a teacher at school was asking me a question that he didn't expect me to answer. I swallowed and tried to force the words out with confidence, but my voice sounded weak and unsure. "He is fighting."

"Do you want to speak to him?"

"Yes," I said, my anger instantly melting at the thought of talking to Mohammad. "But how can I? He's at the border fighting the Iraqis."

"I can help you, but you must be strong."

"Why? What happened?" I tried to imagine what was wrong. Images of Mohammad's helicopter crashing down in Iraqi territory filled my mind. I saw Mohammad captured, beaten, imprisoned. I saw him dying in a hospital bed, surrounded by soldiers. But how could I talk to him? It didn't make sense.

"There was a problem with his car." As soon as my uncle started speaking, my mother was by my side. I felt her take Daniel from me. "You must be strong, Annahita. What I am about to tell you will not be easy for you to hear." My uncle motioned for me to sit down, but I waved him away. My legs had stopped working anyway—I could feel no part of my body, just a giant, choking mass in my chest and throat. My uncle swallowed and carried on. "The morning he left you he was driving on the freeway when a car merged and hit him. Mohammad was trapped in the wreckage, and it took hours to cut him free. They took him to hospital, and he called for Hussein and his own brother. He said that the doctors were telling him he just needed a little blood, but he knew he was in a bad way. He asked them to take care of you both. Later that night he fell into a coma, and he's been like that ever since. I can take you to see him in the hospital now."

When the news hit me, it was as if all the fear and all the sorrow and all the pain of the world had been woven together just for me. The choking feeling grew stronger, and I feared I would not be able to breathe.

Anger mixed with fear. My family had tried to protect me, assuming that Mohammad would soon pull through just as the doctors said he would. But the time for pretending was over. Hope was running out.

I felt hands on my arms and shoulders gently steer me out toward the car. The city was quiet as we drove across it. I stared out at the streets I had known all my life, but they looked like strangers to me. Then there was a hospital garden, lined with low trees and a wide pool. And then I was in the foyer of the hospital. The place was full of faces I knew, and in that moment I could not understand why so many people from my family would be there at the same time.

Two guards stood at the entrance to a ward farther in the hospital. I don't remember anything that was said to them, but as soon as they stepped aside my uncle placed his arm around my shoulder and spoke in soft, low tones. "When they found him the steering wheel had driven into his abdomen. His legs were broken, and his face was badly cut by the windshield. He does not look like you remember him."

The ward was big, with white metal beds lining the walls on either side beneath tall windows. I thought we had entered the ward by mistake at first, for I could not recognize any of the men in the beds as Mohammad. But my uncle's hands steered me over to the far corner, where two doctors were standing beside a man whose face was covered with blood and bandages.

What I could see of Mohammad's body was enough to terrify me. There was barely a single patch of his skin that was not cut or bruised, and his hand lay broken and bandaged at the side. Drips and machines stood all around, and in his mouth I could see that his tongue was cut and badly swollen. But it was his eyes that were the worse. Though they bore no sign of injury, they were open, staring lifelessly at the ceiling.

I had never seen anyone in a coma before, and I tried to gently rouse him by placing my hand on his shoulder and telling him that it was time to wake up. He didn't move. He just stared up, right through me, his chest barely rising which each tiny breath that he took.

Immediately I felt the need to pray. I cried out, calling on God, every imam, and anyone else I could think of to make Mohammad better. If anyone could help, I would devote myself to their service for the rest of my life.

It was May, and the sun was already warm in the early mornings. I sat in the garden the next day, waiting for visiting time to begin. When the guards finally let me pass, I was the first into the ward, Hussein following quickly behind me.

Mohammad looked no different on that second day. I sat in silence beside him for what felt like hours. Eventually I was aware there were doctors standing around him, talking to Hussein.

"He needs medicine that we don't have," they said. "There is a risk that he will develop a blood clot in the lung, and we need to thin his blood urgently."

"Why don't you find it?" said Hussein.

"The war. All of our supplies are low, and many have run out."

I let the conversation carry on without me. I was staring at Mohammad, looking at his eyes again and holding his hand. "Come back, please," I whispered. "Come back and see your child. Come back to both of us."

It was the smallest twitch at first, so small that I thought I had imagined it. But it happened again as I stared; one of his fingers pressed itself into my hand. "Mohammad?" He twitched again, and I knew he could hear me. "Would you like to see your son? Shall I bring Daniel here?" Again the twitch. I looked back at his face and saw a tear well up in his eye.

I made Hussein drive as fast as he could back home. My mom looked shocked when I told her that Mohammad was waking up, but there was no time to stop and answer her questions. I ran back to the car with Daniel in my arms, desperate to get back to Mohammad.

We were back at the hospital less than an hour after we left, but the guards would not let us in. "It is no longer visiting time," they said. "You cannot go in."

I tried all I could, but it was no use.

We sat in the garden for a while, until Hussein suggested that he drive Daniel and me back to our home to get some of Mohammad's things. Reluctantly, I agreed.

As we pulled onto the street outside our home, I saw military vehicles parked nearby, and I began to worry. I walked up toward the door, but in front of it were a handful of Mohammad's friends that I recognized. They were all in uniform. Some of them were crying. What did they know that I didn't know? Hadn't I just come from the hospital?

"I'm sorry," one of them said. "He's dead."

When someone dies in Iran, things happen quickly. People are notified straight away. They gather that day, and the body is normally buried by sunset. Perhaps the crowds and the speed with which things happen are a comfort to some people. To me, they only added to the pain.

I cried all the way from our house back to Mohammad's parents' house. Deep sobs and wordless cries came from my mouth, and I held Daniel closer than I had ever held him. But as soon as I walked into the home where I had been married just one year earlier, something changed.

It was evening, and the house was full of people. There was nowhere to sit down, no place to get away from the crowds. Everywhere I looked people were sobbing, and every pair of eyes stared back at me, probing me, expecting me to share my own tears with them. All I could taste was acid in my mouth. All I could hear was the noise of people's grief.

My tears dried up that night.

There were none in my eyes when I woke the following day either.

"We have to go to the grave," my mom said quietly as she entered my bedroom. "You need to wear these."

I looked blankly at the black clothes she was holding. They made no sense to me. My mind felt muddled. Why would I wear them? And why would I go to a grave? With our first-year

wedding anniversary coming up Mohammad and I were planning a party. It was going to be such a good party, with a house
full of guests and dancing that would go on all night. He had
ordered some new clothes, and they were waiting to be collected
from the boutique. "I can't go to a grave," I said. "I have to pick
up Mohammad's new suit."

When I came out of the room I remembered what it had felt
like the night before. People were sobbing everywhere I looked. I
stared back at them. It was confusing to me. Why would so many
people be acting this way?

I drifted through the drive to the grave as though I were
heading somewhere else entirely. As we stood there, surrounded
by concrete and flags and photographs of people I had never seen
before, my only thought was how strange it all was to be standing there like that.

It got stranger when we drove back to Mohammad's parents' home. There was a photograph of Mohammad outside the
house, and the sight of it shocked me. Suddenly the sound of
weeping was the only sound I could hear. Strangers reached out
to grab and hug me. My head felt heavy, and my eyes struggled
to hold on to any one thing.

"Why is his wife not crying?" I heard someone say. "Is she
not sorry? Did she not love him? Is she happy that he's gone?"

The sound of people's crying was bad, but the silence that snaked
through my parents' house was worse. People stepped carefully
as they moved from room to room, their eyes cast down. They
covered their bodies in black clothes. There was no music. There

were no sounds of laughter, no heat rising as a room full of people danced and danced until the laughter overcame them. Instead, there was nothing. And into that void my confusion grew, and my thoughts grew louder and louder.

Why were people behaving this way?

Was it some cruel game they were playing?

Why did they all want me to cry and weep and wail when all I wanted to do was scream at them to stop?

And where was Mohammad?

I was like a child staring into a room through misty glass. I knew that something was happening around me, but I could not fully comprehend it. All it took in those early days was one concerned look or a gentle hand on my shoulder, and I would spend hours bound by panic. My thoughts became like the winds before a thunderstorm. They hurled themselves around within me. They stung like a swarm of angry wasps. Sometimes I feared the raging would never stop.

When the panic did subside, I would return to the one thing that I could understand in it all: Daniel. I could still give him what he needed. The times when I was feeding or changing him or holding him so close that his warmth and his smell filled my senses, they were the only times that I ever came close to remembering what life was like before all this panic and darkness descended.

I looked at the clock one afternoon. It was nearly two. My mind was filled with memories of the last day I had seen Mohammad. I recalled how Daniel had spent the day crying, and I had spent the day with my eyes constantly returning to the clock, willing the hands to edge around until the time when Mohammad would return. Two o'clock. That was the time he always came home. Always.

I held Daniel tight as I ran out of the house and into the street. I looked for cars, but there were none driving on the road. I searched those that were parked, but they were all empty. I shouted Mohammad's name, wondering if he had somehow gotten lost and forgotten where to find my parents' house, but no reply came. Where could he be? Which way would he come from? I looked about me, desperate. The only person I saw was Khanoum. She was at my side. Her arm was across my back. She was crying.

———

One time I found my mom holding Mohammad's razor and toothbrush, which he had kept at their house for the times when we stayed over. She said that she was going to give them away to the poor, as was the custom.

"Why would you do that?" I asked. "He will need them again when he comes back."

I felt her fingers dig into the flesh at the top of my arms. It hurt.

"He's not coming back!" she said. Her voice was so loud that it hurt too. But I still did not understand fully. I stared back at her. I felt numb.

She started to shake me. "Wake up! Why can't you see? It's enough we don't have Mohammad. We can't lose you as well."

———

In Iran the tradition is for a widow to dress in black for the first four months after her husband's death. Never once in all that time did I wear any of the clothes my mom laid out for me. How could I? To do so would be to admit that the game was real.

Instead I tried in my own way to change what was going on. I would stand outside the house every day at two o'clock, watching. Sometimes I would be holding a plate of Mohammad's favorite food. A plate of rice whose wisps of cloud rising above it smelled so sweetly of saffron. A glass of black tea spiced with cardamon and cinnamon. A fresh pomegranate.

They would let me stand there for a while. Eventually, someone would come from inside the house and gently guide me back in. I never knew what became of the food.

———

The one thing that I knew for sure was that I had to make my life about Daniel. I had to care for him. I had to keep him alive. I knew that staying at my parents' house was no good, and every day I begged them to let me take my son back to the home Mohammad and I had rented. I told them that the sadness of their own home was not good for either Daniel or me. I pleaded that it was only back in my own home that life could return to normal for me, that I could shake this fog hanging over me.

Eventually, they relented.

Four months had passed since Mohammad's accident, and I was pleased to see that my mom no longer tried to offer me the black clothes of a grieving widow. We drove along the freeway in silence. Daniel was asleep on my lap.

As soon as my dad opened the door of the house, the air

was wrenched from my lungs. I stumbled, almost falling to my knees. But I had to go inside. I was compelled to go in, even though every step filled me with horror.

His shoes by the door. His bag on the floor. His glass of water by his side of the bed.

A bomb exploded within me. There was no way of stopping the tears. Even if I had wanted to, I could not stop. I could not stop. I could only weep and feel my face pressed up against the rug on the floor of our bedroom, inhaling what little air that I could between the sobs and the tears and the agony that had twisted itself into every part of my insides. That was all I could do. That was all there was in the world.

———

I stopped fighting the truth after that visit back to the house. I woke up from the state that I had been in for four months. But this new world that my eyes were suddenly open to was so much worse. No amount of silence or sobbing or black clothes could ever begin to release the pain I was feeling inside.

Food held no interest for me. I became sick and stopped sleeping. My parents did everything for Daniel, feeding and washing him and taking him to the doctors when he got a fever. I was only aware of one thing—the great weight within my chest that suffocated me from the inside out. Day by day, I could feel myself fall apart.

When I found the cassette with the song about the poppy, I played it over and over. The words spoke right to the deepest part of my sorrow.

I am so very alone.

My life is like you. When you die, I die, so very soon.

40

—

Though my grieving was just beginning, other people's mourning was over. Mohammad's family wanted to follow tradition and give away their son's possessions to the poor, and since I could not bear the thought of them throwing away anything that reminded me of Mohammad, I went back to the house to join them as they sorted through his things.

The shock was lesser on this second visit, but the pain was just as fierce. As I walked from room to room I had such vivid memories of time with Mohammad. I remembered the way that Mohammad would pick Daniel up and hold his tiny face next to his own. They looked so alike, and I used to laugh as Mohammad would match his face to Daniel's, either taking on a tired scowl or a blissful milky sleep. "It's a copy, but an original too!" he'd say.

Mohammad's uniform reminded me of the time he told me about being captured in Iraq. He was with a handful or other men, and they were locked in a room. Mohammad guessed that they wouldn't make it out alive, so he encouraged everyone to write letters to their loved ones. They were freed after a day or two, but I liked the idea of him calming the fears of his men by telling them to face death in such a way. But it was a bitter memory—I never did get to see what he wrote to me.

We had not even been married for a year when Mohammad died, and packing up our home was over so quickly. I stood outside and looked at the cars with their doors open and a few scattered boxes and bags littering their back seats. It was too little to show for a loss so great.

—

In the four months since Mohammad died, the world around me had changed beyond recognition. In May I was a wife with a newborn baby and thoughts about our first wedding anniversary looming, but in November I emerged without a husband into a world where fourteen-year-old boys patrolled the streets with AK-47s.

Though Khomeini had taken power at the start of the year, it was only as winter settled over the country that the real changes became clear. The shock of those changes was the only thing powerful enough to cut through my grieving.

I was so deeply troubled by the sights that greeted me as I accompanied my sister or mom when they walked to the market. The mosque near my parents' house became a military base, and from behind its walls everyone could hear the sound of teenage boys being trained to use rifles. In front of its gates the boys would gather, their weapons too big for the smaller ones among them and hung low about their waists. It only seemed to make them more determined to prove their power, and it was these young boys who were the worst. They would step into the path of women as they walked and point at their chadors with their rifles, chastising them for showing too much flesh or some other crime. Soon these gangs of armed boys would appear at our doors, too, reminding all residents of their duty as good Muslims to attend the mosque daily.

Mohammad had hated what the revolution stood for. When Khomeini first came to power he imposed a curfew from 9 p.m. to 6 a.m., with roadblocks in place to catch offenders. Mohammad had been late coming back from his military base one night and was turned back by some men guarding one of the roads near our part of the city. He had tried to persuade them to let him pass, telling them that he had been fighting their war in Iraq and just wanted to get home to his pregnant wife, but they had refused. Eventually, he found a different way back, parking the car down a side street and jumping over walls to get back to us. By the time he eased open the door it was almost midnight. I lay in bed and listened as he ranted and raged at the way the country was changing. I stared in shock as he opened the window, filled his lungs with air and shouted into the darkness, "I hope Khomeini gets hanged!"

By the time November came around, nobody would ever dream of doing such a foolish thing. In addition to recruiting teenage boys, the regime had established a new military force designed to protect the Islamic ideals of the country. They were known as the Sepah, and they struck terror into people's hearts.

I first saw them one morning as I was walking with my mom. I heard the sound of an engine running hard and braking suddenly. I looked up to see a patrol car cutting the road off and two women and two men descending upon a woman. She was screaming out for help, but nobody moved. Everyone, myself included, just watched as the four guards pulled her to the ground and then dragged her into the back of the vehicle. As soon as the doors closed her screams were silenced.

"Don't stare!" hissed my mom as the guards drove back down the road in our direction. I did not lift my eyes from the ground until we got home.

"They've filled the regime with the unemployed and the homeless!" shouted my dad when we got home and told him about what we had seen. "They're no good for this country. These fanatics will ruin us all. Did you hear about what they did to cousin Hamid? They caught him putting up posters in the street and threw him in jail. Nobody's seen him for a week, and whenever his brother asks about him he's just told that Hamid is a Communist and has some questions to answer. Nobody will tell them where he is or what he is being charged with."

And so my life divided neatly in two. One part of my life was dominated by grief for Mohammad, the other by fear of what was happening in Iran. Sometimes things swapped over, and I grieved the darkness that had fallen on my homeland and feared the prospect of life without my son's father. Whichever way around these feelings were, the outcome was always the same, and I felt weaker with every passing month.

———

I had walked to the market alone one day when I first saw the crane. I had been quietly filling my basket with vegetables and fruit when I noticed that everyone else in the market was standing still. I followed their gazes and looked up and saw it: a crane parked in the middle of the street. From it there hung a man's body. His neck was held by a noose. His arms had been tied behind his back, his eyes covered with a blindfold.

I started shaking as soon as I saw the body. When I finally was able to look away, I saw that others were shaking too. As I turned and left I saw one of the teenage boys with a rifle. "This man sold drugs. Today we have brought justice. Allahu Akbar!" I kept my eyes low and hurried home.

I STOOD IN THE COURT AND TRIED TO make my voice sound strong. "I am seventeen years and eight months," I said.

The oldest of the three mullahs looked at me, raised his eyebrows, and consulted with the other two. "Then you are too young to file a report," he said, finally. "Your father-in-law must file it instead of you."

I sat down again. I tried not to look over at the man who sat slumped at the side of the room. He was the one who had driven his car into Mohammad's, but I had not come to the court for revenge. I had come because Mohammad's brother and sister told me that I had to.

In the months after Mohammad's death I had done more and more things that his brother and sister had told me to. I had started to dress Daniel the way they liked and to take him to the doctor they knew on their side of the city, rather than the clinic my family used. Every week, two or three times, I served tea and food to them when they visited my parents' house.

I didn't mind the mullah's directive to return to court accompanied by my father-in-law. Mohammad's father was a kind man. I liked to sit and watch him hold Daniel. Knowing that he was around brought a degree of security and protection. Dressing

Daniel in clothes I didn't like or traveling across the city to visit a doctor was a small price to pay for something as valuable as that.

As we left the court, Mohammad's sister leaned toward me. "We will be back here soon for another matter," she said, quietly.

"Why?" I asked.

"My family should be looking after Daniel, not you. Don't you think a mullah would agree that a grandfather's rights are more important than those of a teenage girl?"

I knew she was right, and the thought horrified me.

A month later we stood in the same court, and this time I was unable to keep control of my voice. I wept as the mullah told me that I was still too young to speak for myself and that Daniel's grandfather was to be consulted on every matter relating to his care. But, for now, he said that I could keep Daniel.

Even though Mohammad's father assured me that he was happy with the arrangement, his son and daughter were not. They refused to accept the mullah's ruling and vowed to return to court again. Had it not been for the fact that Mohammad's father died of a heart attack six months later, they might have gotten their way.

Instead, I was left with the knowledge that nobody could take Daniel away from me any longer, as well as the grief of losing the last person on earth who knew and loved Mohammad like I did.

———

My whole world had become about taking care of Daniel, and I was grateful for the fact that my fear of losing him had slowly drawn me out of my grief and sharpened my senses. The longer the regime was in power, the more I became aware of the fact that there was danger all around, not just from Mohammad's family.

Life had not been easy for women since the revolution. Anyone found outside without a black chador pulled tight and far down over her head would be inviting harassment from any mullah, official, or devoted follower of Islam who wanted to demonstrate their religious purity to anyone watching. If we tried to go outside without a husband, father, or brother by our side we could face all manner of questions.

I became a prisoner in my parents' home. If Hussein or my father couldn't accompany me when I wanted to go out, I was stuck. When I complained to my father, his only solution was for me to stay at home.

Things got worse soon after I turned eighteen. Khomeini ruled that every widow could marry a second time without bringing shame on the man. He also declared that each man could marry up to four women.

Almost overnight my prison was breached. The husband of one of my cousins visited me and asked if I wanted to marry him. I was so angry that he would suggest such a thing. I told him that I loved my cousin and would never treat her that way. He simply shrugged and left the house, as if the whole conversation had been nothing more than a failed transaction for a car or a piece of furniture.

Despite my anger I kept the conversation from my parents. I knew that I was a burden on them and that, like almost every man in Iran, my father was struggling to know how to protect his family from the new regime.

I chose to keep the second proposal of marriage a secret too. This time it was from my neighbor. He walked into our court-yard one day when I sat alone watching Daniel gather stones from the flower bed and pile them up at my feet.

The neighbor was older than my own father and had a belly

that was as fat as mine had been when I was pregnant. He cleared his throat and told me that he would be willing to marry me. "I will restore your honor," he said. I looked back at him and felt the bile rise within me.

"The only thing I am willing to do with you is chop off your head." The words were out of my mouth before I knew it. His eyes bulged, and his face twisted. Within seconds he was gone. It took hours for me to calm down.

My problem was not just my own concern. Whenever my uncle visited, he and my father would argue about "what to do with Annahita." It did not matter whether I was in the same room as them or not; they still carried on as if I was deaf and mute. My uncle would say that there were people talking about me, saying that I was bringing shame on the family by remaining unmarried. My father would counter that I was happy at home and that there was no need to change anything. My uncle would urge my father to see sense and find me a husband as soon as he could. Soon they would both be shouting.

All I wanted was to be safe. It was clear to me that my father could not be expected to provide that for both Daniel and me. So I made up my mind. If I could find the right man, I would marry again. Not for love and not to try and erase the memory of Mohammad. I would marry for safety, nothing else.

—

When I first heard about him, Asghar sounded like the perfect fit. A friend of Mohammad's visited and told me about him. He said that he was a soldier, just like Mohammad, and he even knew my husband a little when they served together. Asghar had been married before, and like me he had a child from that marriage. His wife had even died in a car crash. It had been four months since he had lost her and, with his daughter still in the hospital with her injuries, he needed help.

I was nineteen and a half years old and had just celebrated Daniel's second birthday. In the two years that had passed a lot had changed for me, but I could so easily remember the agony of grief in those first few months. Even before I met Asghar, I felt compassion for him.

I talked with my parents, and they agreed that he should come to visit our house and allow us all to meet him.

He was older than Mohammad, and at least ten years older than me. He was tall and thin as a post, but his eyes were what interested me. I thought that I saw in them a little of the same pain that I had lived with for so long.

"Would you want to marry me?" he asked as soon as we were left alone. It was impossible for me not to remember how different this same conversation had been with Mohammad. He had made me laugh and told me enough about himself for me to trust him entirely. Asghar was the opposite. To my mind he was weighted down by grief. Laughter and vulnerability were just not possible at a time like that.

"I have no feelings about you, and I don't want a man to be intimate with. But I do want a home for my child. I want to be safe. Can you understand that?"

He nodded. "I want the same thing too, just to live as friends. Perhaps things might change later on, but for now I want to do exactly as you say."

"I am glad." I smiled. So did he. He looked younger when he smiled. He looked like a different man.

An unmarried couple would never live together in Iran back then, so since we were both looking for help and stability in the day-to-day, we agreed to marry soon. When I told my parents that the wedding would be in two weeks, neither of them were entirely happy, but I wondered whether secretly they were both relieved as well.

Asghar introduced me to his daughter, Cherie. She had been badly injured in the accident, fracturing her skull. She was one year old, and the doctors had spoken of possible damage to her brain. I thought she was beautiful, just like an angel. I knew that I could help her. I knew that I could take care of her.

There was so much to talk about, and Asghar wanted to know about Daniel and what life had been like for me since Mohammad died. He asked how much Mohammad's pension was and how much other money I had. I told him that all the pension money went into an account for Daniel that my dad was in charge of. Asghar said he thought that was odd.

My dad was angry when I told him about the conversation. "You cannot trust that man," he said.

I defended Asghar, but I wondered all the same.

"Why do you need to know about my money?" I asked him the next time he brought it up.

He held his hands wide and apologized immediately. "Annahita, I am so sorry. If I ever do anything wrong, it's because I'm still so sad from losing my wife. All you ever need to do is tell me, and I will change whatever I need to change about myself."

That was enough for me. I felt such sympathy for Asghar. I knew exactly what he had been through, and I understood just how hard it could be to think clearly when grief has its tightest grip on you. "It's okay," I said. "We will be okay."

———

The wedding was simple. There was none of the ceremony that had mattered so much when I married Mohammad; no desperate search for the perfect dress, no quiet conversation with my dad outside the house as we waited for my new parents to arrive to collect me. There was just a car full of my and Daniel's possessions taken over to Asghar's house on that morning.

The mullah married us and left soon after. My parents and the rest of my family stayed for a meal. I don't remember what we ate, but I know that soon my parents were talking about being tired and wanting to go home.

My family gone, I sat next to my new husband and looked about me at his relatives. They felt like strangers to me, but I hoped that in time that might change. Daniel would grow to know them all, and I hoped they would love him back.

I automatically flinched when Asghar placed his hand on mine. His grip was tight, and he held mine in place. "And now we're going to bed!" he announced to the room, pulling me to my feet. There were smiles and a murmur of approval. I wanted to pull back my hand and tell him that this was not what we had agreed to, but standing there in a room of strangers I lost my voice.

When he closed the door behind us I spoke up. "I asked you to promise that you would not touch me. Why are you doing this?"

When it came, the first blow to my face caused more shock than pain.

The second slap was the one that hurt.

And it was the third that knocked me to the floor.

"Why? You promised, Asghar!"

The silence hovered between us. Asghar was breathing heavily. I could taste blood in my mouth. My cheek felt as though it had been stung by a hundred needles.

"You're my wife. I can do anything that I want."

Then he forced himself upon me.

I LEARNED QUICKLY NOT TO SPEAK TO my parents about Asghar's violence. Whenever I told my mother the truth about where my bruises had come from or why I winced when she embraced me, her anger was such that she could not help herself from reprimanding Asghar. And whenever I heard her chastise him with her words, I knew that as soon as he and I were alone, Asghar would attack me with his fists.

I was not naive. I knew that many wives in Iran were beaten by their husbands. And in the first weeks of our marriage there was a part of me that believed Asghar continued to be deeply affected by his wife's death. After all, I'd tell myself, five months after Mohammad died I was barely able to breathe for crying so hard.

Yet Asghar could breathe all right. He could shout the vilest curses too. He could slap me so hard my ear would wail all through the night. And he could punch so fast and so strong that I thought I might never catch my breath again.

If there was one consolation, it was the fact that he did not hurt Daniel. For one month, Asghar's rages were directed solely at me. My son, it appeared, was invisible to him.

In the end, it was something so trivial that caused Asghar to change. It was late one afternoon, and the house was quiet, the way Asghar liked it. I was sewing the buttons on a dress that I had made for Cherie, and Daniel was sitting down on the carpet, playing with some toy cars and animals. Asghar was reading, though what it was I did not know. I had already learned that it was best not to ask.

I was the first one to notice the damp patch that was slowly creeping across the carpet from beneath Daniel. The carpet was a gift from my parents, and I knew it would not take long to clean up.

"Oh, Daniel!" I cooed softly, sweeping him up in my arms. Daniel strained to be allowed back down to play among his kingdom of cars and monsters but quickly gave in to a fit of giggles as I nuzzled his neck.

"What?" Asghar had already put his book down and was staring at the carpet.

"It's nothing," I said. "I will clean it up once I've changed Daniel."

My words had no affect. Asghar jumped up immediately, walked over to my sewing, and grabbed a needle. Then he turned to me. He crossed the room in three paces and, with one violent twist, pulled Daniel from my arms. Shouldering me out of the way, he walked toward the bedroom.

"What are you doing?" I said, trying so hard to fill my voice with calm. Daniel was crying, looking back at me, arms outstretched over Asghar's shoulder.

"He needs to learn what happens to little boys who pee in the wrong place," Asghar shouted as he pushed me back, slammed shut the door, and flicked the lock.

All pretense of calm vanished as I slammed my fists into

the door. "Asghar! Open the door! Please, Asghar, give me back my son!"

"No!" he shouted back.

Daniel's cries turned into screams. I had never heard him make such a noise.

"Daniel!" I yelled, my hands clawing at the door handle, my shoulder hitting the door. "Daniel!"

I heard the lock turn and watched the handle move. Asghar was standing in the doorway. I pushed past him and ran to Daniel. He was lying curled up tight on the bed, screaming so hard there was no sound coming from his tiny body.

He felt weak in my arms as I scooped him up. I turned to leave. Asghar was still in the doorway. "Why are you trying to stop me?" he said. "Can't you understand that children need discipline? Your father never disciplined you, and you need it now. You're a bad woman."

"He's *my* son, not yours," I shouted back.

"Whore!" he shouted as his hand shot out and connected with the side of my head, just by my eye. "You sleep with every man you see. You deserve all of this."

———

That afternoon marked the beginning of a new level of violence at home. Suddenly it was not only me that Asghar's fists sought out when he got angry, but now Daniel as well. If we were lucky we might go two or three days without one of us being hit, but the shouts and the blows and the pain were never far away.

I could not understand it. A lot of families punished their children in Iran, but Asghar was more violent than any I had heard of before. The only time I ever gained any glimpse of insight into why he behaved in such a way was when he told me that his father had died when he was young and his uncle had taken responsibility for his discipline. But his words were not delivered as a confession or a plea for compassion. Instead, Asghar took pride in his brutal childhood. "This is how I became a man," he would say whenever I held Daniel as he sobbed in my arms, a fresh handprint quickly revealing itself on his bare skin. "It's the way the boy will become one too."

Sometimes I would shout back at him, screaming that Daniel was only two years old. I would get my own handprint for a comment like that.

As the early weeks of our marriage passed, I knew I had a choice to make. Islamic law only allowed a woman to divorce her husband within the first three months of the marriage. After that, only the husband could call for a divorce.

We had married on June 4, and as the end of August approached I agonized over what to do. Of course I wanted to be free from Asghar right from the very first night of our marriage, and ever since Daniel had become a target I had been desperate to keep my boy safe. But divorce was not a guarantee of freedom. In an instant I would return to my previous condition: vulnerable to the lusts of greedy old men and the dishonest young ones. I would have no choice but to return to my state as a visual prisoner in my parents' home—if they would have me. To be not quite twenty years old and twice married already would be a source of great shame. None of my siblings were married at the time, and I knew that the scandal my divorce would cause would ruin any chances they would have of marrying into an upright, respectful family.

It was an agonizing choice, but eventually I made up my mind. I phoned for a taxi early one morning and swept Daniel up in my arms when I heard it pull up outside. I had grown so skilled at shutting the door silently behind me that I was able to leave the house undetected.

Were it not for the sound of the taxi driver's radio I would have gotten away with it. But the music was loud, and by the time I had told the driver my destination and climbed into the back seat, Asghar was standing by the driver's window, leaning in.

"Where are you taking my wife, friend?"

"The courthouse."

"I'll come with you," Asghar said, as happily as if we were all going to the zoo.

As we drove away, I swallowed hard and spoke from the back seat. "I am going to divorce you."

Asghar sat in silence for some minutes. Then, as we approached the courthouse, he turned around and unleashed the vilest torrent of abuse I had ever heard. He said things about me and about my family that made the taxi driver squirm in his seat and turn the radio up.

"It is I who should be divorcing you," he spat. "You are the one who has brought pain into this marriage. It is me who has been hurt by you, not the other way around."

He turned back to watch the road. Even though I had tried to become deaf to his cruel words in the previous months, they still shocked me. But I chose to put them out of my mind and think about what I was about to do. Soon I would be able to leave

Asghar and his violence behind me. Soon I would be able to start life again, no matter how uncertain or difficult it might be.

I stepped from the taxi and made my way to the court. Asghar fell in beside me. He was smiling. He never smiled.

"If you go inside I will follow you. I will tell them that you've been with other men. I will find two witnesses, and they will confirm it."

I stopped walking. I looked at him carefully. Never once had he shown any fear of hurting either me or Daniel. Never once had he shown any sign of genuine regret for causing us pain. I knew that he was not afraid of lying to the court. And I knew that if he did that, there would only be one possible outcome for me.

I had never seen a woman being stoned before, but I had read enough newspaper reports and seen enough footage on the television to know that it is a terrible way to die. You are bound at the ankles, as well as your wrists and your elbows, which are pulled tight behind your back. You are then buried up to your waist while people throw rocks at you. If you are lucky a rock will make you lose consciousness early on. Either way, though, death comes slowly.

Since the revolution, stoning had become the punishment for a woman caught in adultery. For a man, it was only a couple of lashes with a whip if he was found guilty.

I thought about the gossip that I had heard about myself ever since Mohammad had died, how people were saying that it was my fault, that God was punishing me. Perhaps they were right. Perhaps death was what I deserved. But I had a choice, and I knew that if I was going to die, I would not let it be at the hand of a mob of angry strangers.

I looked at Asghar, turned my back on the courthouse, and headed back home.

Asghar took strength from my decision to return home that day. He knew he had even more power over me and that I was weak. As a result, his attacks grew more frequent and more fierce.

It wasn't just the physical violence that increased. If Daniel stirred at night or made too much noise in the evening, Asghar would shout at him to go to sleep, and Daniel would run, his eyes wide in terror, to his bed. He would be so quiet and still it was sometimes hard to tell if he was still breathing.

Asghar played with me like a cat with a wounded bird, tormenting me just for fun. One day I walked into the bedroom to find him ripping from my photo albums any picture I had of Mohammad. "You and that foolish husband," he sneered as he peeled back each photo before holding it up and carefully tearing it into tiny pieces.

All I could do was watch and cry.

Even though Asghar and Mohammad were both in the army, Mohammad was often away during our year of marriage, but Asghar never went to fight. He was in the military and was permanently in Isfahan training other soldiers. Only once did he go away, and those two weeks when he was up north near Kurdistan were like an oasis of peace for Daniel and me, as well as his daughter Cherie who had finally left the hospital and was now living with us.

Two things happened during that fortnight.

I discovered his first wife's diary and read what she had

written about how unhappy she was in the marriage and how violent he was with her. Instead of giving me comfort or making me feel as though I was not alone, reading her words only made me feel more trapped. Death was clearly the only way out.

The other event was a visit from my aunt. Asghar had stopped my family from coming to see me at home, so when I opened the door and saw her, I wept with relief. She cried too, but her tears were born of shock.

"What happened to you?" She looked me up and down, her hands holding me carefully as if fingering the thinnest, most fragile glass. "Where are these bruises from? And your skin? You look like an old woman."

"I have not been well," I said. "My diet has not been so good, and I've not been sleeping either." She knew I was lying, but even though she tried to help me, as soon as Asghar returned, bringing his violence with him, my aunt finally realized how powerless she was.

———

I suppose it was almost inevitable that I would try to kill myself. I tried soon after Asghar returned. Valium was so easily available in Iran back then, and I already had more than enough on hand. I decided to take some at night, go to bed, and never wake up. What I didn't count on was how thin I had become and how quickly a handful of pills would get to work. By the time I had swallowed them all in the kitchen and prepared to go to bed, I was feeling dizzy.

The next thing I knew I was in the hospital. Someone gave me some more medicine, and someone else told me I could go home. The rest of the day was a daze, and even though I was back in person, a part of me was lost.

———

I fell pregnant after our first anniversary, about the same time that Asghar's sister came to live with us. I hoped that my pregnancy or her presence might distract Asghar a little, but in the end it only made things worse. His sister had a boyfriend in the city and would call him on our phone when Asghar was out.

A month after she moved in with us, the boyfriend phoned one day when Asghar's sister was out with their mother, a sour-faced woman called Ziynab. As soon as the call ended Asghar started at me. "Who was that?"

"Your sister's boyfriend."

"That's impossible. You're a liar. It must have been your boy-friend, whore! That's why you're pregnant!"

I tried to explain, but he would not listen.

He was still raging when his sister and mother came back. "She says you have a boyfriend," Asghar said to his sister as soon as she walked in.

She looked scared but denied it fully. "It must be hers," she said, pointing at me.

At that, the air filled with more shouting than I had ever heard in that house. Ziynab was screaming at me, Daniel and Cherie wailed in their beds, and Asghar yelled that he would finally kill me.

He disappeared outside and came back with a length of plas-tic hose about as long as his arm. He hit me all over my body with it, swinging his arm back as the hose flew high into the air before coming crashing down on me. I tried to shield the blows with my arms, but it made little difference. The hose bit deep into my flesh, burning like a hot iron straight from the fire. My whole body was in agony, and I crawled like an animal toward the kitchen as yet more blows landed on my back.

I managed to lock the door behind me and curl up on the floor. I tried to tell my mind to focus on the feel of the cold tiles against my cheek, but it was no use. Every part of me was on fire. Every inch of my flesh cried out.

There was a pane of glass at the top of the door. It exploded and rained down onto me. I tried to cover my head from the worst of it but soon heard Asghar scrambling through. He had a shovel in his hand and swung it over and over on me.

I thought I would die right there on the floor. Ziynab and his sister were standing over me and managed to stop Asghar for a while.

"I want to help you," said Ziynab. "But you must tell the truth."

"I am telling you the truth," I begged. "She has a boyfriend. You can phone the telephone exchange if you like and get the number and find him for yourself."

For some reason Asghar agreed to this. He stood, his ear close to mine, shovel in hand, as I crawled out of the kitchen and to the phone. I tried as best I could to explain to the operator what was going on, and after some time he said he had the phone records in front of him.

"The last number that called, was it from Isfahan?"

"Yes," he said.

"And can you see any calls to that number from this phone?"

We waited in silence as the man checked. Asghar's sister hid her face in her hands, but Asghar and his mother would only stare at me. The pain increased as I shifted the phone from one hand to the other.

The operator replied. "Yes, I can see many calls."

"When did they start?"

"About a month ago."

I looked at Asghar. Surely this proved it. He grabbed the phone from me. "You're not a real man!" he shouted. "I'm going to come and kill you!"

I braced myself for more attacks from the shovel, hoping that death would not be far behind. But no blows came. Instead Ziynab sat by me on the floor.

"Why do you want to make a big thing out of something so small like this?"

"Your son hurt me." It was all I could say.

She looked at me like I was no older than Daniel. "It is normal for a woman to be beaten by her husband. That is how women learn."

She left me then. With each breath the pain got worse. I feared for the life of the baby inside me, and I feared for my own life too. I didn't know how I could survive. After everything he had done, how could I live? Even if he didn't come back in and attack me again with the shovel, how could I hope to still be alive in another year?

When he came back into the room, Asghar sounded strange. He knelt opposite me and made me look at his face. Though his voice was soft and quiet, his eyes were just as hard as ever. "I promise that I won't hurt you again," he said. "I'm angry with myself. I don't know why I did that to you. May God forgive me."

He stood up and left.

I knew this was not the end of Asghar's violence. I knew he

would hurt me again. Would God forgive him? I had no idea. I had long since given up trying to understand the way God worked. God was a mystery to me. With my life the way it was, I had no appetite for puzzles.

———

Somehow, the baby I was carrying survived the beatings. When she was born she cried as though she wanted the whole world to wake up. We named her Roksana, and after her arrival Asghar's attacks lessened a little but never so much that I could fully relax. He was a hair trigger, a bomb waiting to explode at the slightest twitch of movement.

So when he came home one afternoon and ran into the bedroom, I expected the worst. I put Roksana down on the bed and prepared to take whatever punches he was going to throw at me.

None came. Instead, he said the words that I never imagined I would hear him say.

"I'm leaving."

A thousand questions flooded my mind, but my instincts told me to stay quiet and let him be. He was filling a bag with clothes, but when Cherie walked in and stared at him, he stopped.

"The Sepah is going to come for me. They'll kill me. You have to go too. Go and live with my mother. Take Cherie with you."

In all the confusion I did at least have some clarity. I knew that living with his mother was a terrible idea, that life with the woman who believed I deserved to be beaten simply for being alive was not something I wanted my children to experience. Daniel was already terrified of her, and I knew he would only be damaged by her.

"Why are they after you? What happened?"

"A few of us refused to put up the Islamic flag this morning. They think we're staging a coup. I'm going to Turkey and will send for you when it's safe."

Safe. The word had almost lost its meaning to me. I imagined what life would be like without Asghar. I imagined what it would feel like to hear the opening of the door and not sense the fear rise within me. I wondered what it would be like for my children to live in a house where they could run and shout and laugh and make all kinds of mess without fear of Asghar's hand knocking them to the floor. I imagined what it would be like to climb into bed at night without the knowledge that I might again be used for the pleasure of a man who only wanted me dead.

It was a dream so precious that I dared not speak for fear of breaking its spell. It was a butterfly's wing, a single thread from a spider.

In seconds, it was gone.

What would happen when the Sepah came looking for him? Would they just let me carry on and live my life in peace? No. I knew they would throw me in jail without so much as a trial. If I let Asghar leave me in Iran, I would become their target. I would never be safe. Could I be sure that these three children who depended on me for their lives could ever survive? If I tried to live on my own with them I'd be in the same position as I was before, only worse: on my own, running from the regime, totally vulnerable and with three children dependent on me, not just one.

And so, even though it made me physically sick to speak the words out loud, I made Asghar stop and look at me.

"Asghar," I begged. "Please take me with you."

PART TWO

TURKEY

ASGHAR PUT THE PHONE DOWN AND
stared at me. For the longest time there was silence between us.
"He said he'll make a deal."

"So we can go? The children too? We can all go?"

"Yes. But it will cost us."

I dared not ask how much. Asghar picked up the phone and
dialed again, this time talking to his mother. He told her just a
little of what had happened and why he had to leave, and he told
her that he needed money. The figure he mentioned was colossal,
enough to buy our house outright. There was a lot of shouting.

I had half an hour to pack. I stood and stared at the empty
suitcase, my mind stalling.

"Just take what they need," Asghar said as he filled his own
bag. I realized then that I had forgotten where we were going.
Had he said Turkey? Or was it Pakistan or Armenia? I didn't
want to ask, so I just put a couple of outfits for each of the children and myself into the bag.

We were due to meet Asghar's contact in Tehran the next
day, but Asghar wanted us to get out of the house as soon as
possible. He also wanted to leave his car at home, so we took a
taxi over to my parents' house.

"What do we tell them?" I asked.

"Who?"

"My parents. What do we say to them?"

He looked at me dismissively. "I don't care what they know."

"But if we tell them where we have gone and the Sepah come looking for us there, they'll have to lie. I don't want them to get in trouble."

He shrugged. "Tell them what you want then."

And so I did. My parents started fussing over the children as soon as we arrived, and Asghar went off to make another phone call. I took my dad to one side and tried to talk as if everything I was telling him was true. "Asghar has been thinking for a while about moving away, and he says that this is a good time to go now. So we're leaving tomorrow."

"Is this a joke? Where are you moving to?"

"Turkey."

"Turkey? You've got passports?"

"No."

"Then why go to Turkey? If you go without passports you can never come back, you know? You leave here like that, and we'll never see you in Iran again. Is that what you want?"

I fought the urge to cry so hard. "No, Dad," I said. "That's not what I want. But Asghar says this is a good time to go."

"He's wrong. At least wait and get a passport. If money's a problem you can sell your things and stay with us. We can help you."

"No, Dad, we don't have time to wait a year to get passports. We have to go now."

Asghar arrived in the doorway. He looked mad, his eyes burning at me. "I want to talk with you," he said, turning and heading back outside. Dad puffed his cheeks and walked off to find Mom.

"The smuggler says we can only take one of the children."

"No," I said, panicking. "When you spoke to him before he said we could take them all."

"He said he'd make a deal; he didn't say we could take them all. Anyway, I've spoken with him, and he won't change his mind. I'm leaving Cherie with my mom. You're leaving Daniel."

"No! Let me bring both of them. Roksana's so small she hardly counts, and Daniel's still only four so he won't be any trouble."

Asghar grabbed my arm tight. I could feel his fingernails biting through my clothes, feel my arm grow hot, heavy, and numb.

"No," he spat. "Leave the boy, or I'll leave you all behind."

He left me alone in the courtyard then. I felt the same choking feeling in my throat that I remembered from the days of my grief. Only, this time, the pain was even crueler.

"What's wrong?" Mom was walking over to me, holding in her arms my new baby sister she had given birth to a few months earlier. I looked up and saw Dad with her as well. "What is Asghar doing to you? Tell us, please. Why is this happening?"

I sucked down as much air as I could and wiped my eyes. "It's nothing," I said, trying to make my voice sound light and happy as I pushed past them and went back inside.

I took the case and laid it down on the bed. I found Cherie's clothes and laid them to one side. I made another pile of Roksana's and a third of Daniel's. I stared at their two piles. I knew I had to leave him behind, but how could I? It was like trying to gouge one of my own eyes out.

I heard shouting outside the room and went out to check. Asghar was standing in the kitchen, his path blocked by my parents. They turned when they heard me.

"Now he says you're not taking all the children with you? What's going on? This is madness."

I tried to find my calm voice again. "We have to change our plans, Dad. We're going to leave Cherie with his mom and send for her when we're settled."

"And what about Daniel and Roksana?" said Mom, her voice like acid. "Have you grown tired of them too?"

"No, Mom, it's not like that. We just—"

"Life has not been easy for us," Asghar interrupted. "So we need to start again somewhere new. Iran is no good since Khomeini came in. You know that."

"Yes," shouted Dad, "life has not been easy for any of us, but we're not running away on a whim like you are. We're not abandoning our children or cutting off all ties with our homeland. What you are doing is foolish. You'll regret it."

I tried to force a smile. "I know this doesn't make sense to you, but we really want to do this. And it would be so good if you could look after one of the children, just while we get settled. We'll send for them in a few weeks."

"Who?" said Mom. I looked back at her, confused. "Which one do you want to leave with us? Or haven't you even thought that through yet?" She threw her hands up at me.

I knew I had to leave him behind, but saying it was the hardest thing of all. "Daniel," I murmured. At least he would be safe from Asghar, if only for a few weeks. I excused myself, ran to the bathroom, and sobbed and screamed silently into a face full of towels.

———

I hated how light my suitcase felt as I lifted it into the car early the next morning. It spoke of all that had been cut from me. Late the night before Ziynab had come to collect Cherie and take her to a relative somewhere in the city. Saying good-bye to Cherie was the first wound. Then, early in the morning, my dad had told me that I would never see Daniel again. He said that we were wrong to do this, and that even if I ever could get back into the country, he doubted Daniel would ever trust me again. That was the second wound.

The worst was Daniel himself. "You're going to stay here," I said, "with Grandma and Grandpa. You're going to have a holiday with them while Mommy goes to find our new home."

He looked at me and shook his head. "No," he said. "No holiday."

It took everything I had to swallow my feelings down. But I had to, for Daniel and for my parents too. I had to let them think I didn't care about any of this.

That third wound cut so deep it would take decades to heal.

———

Ziynab drove us north. Asghar and I could finally talk freely once we got on the road, but I didn't care to speak. There was nothing to say. I was relieved that I could cry again, and for most of the six hours of the drive between Isfahan and Tehran, that's all I did. As Roksana slept on my lap and my shoulders heaved, Asghar talked with his mother who sat next to him up front about how an escape from the country might be possible.

I listened to them talk about what had gotten Asghar into trouble. I knew it was something to do with him not raising the revolutionary flag, but I didn't know that he had also been overheard telling others how the flag didn't belong on the base at all or that Khomeini's days in power were numbered. And I certainly didn't know that a few of his friends had already been caught and hung for their part in it.

Though we were hundreds of miles away from Isfahan at that point, where the Sepah searching for Asghar were, our arrival in Tehran only brought a new fear. There were members of the regime everywhere, including the Sepah, on what seemed like every street corner. I thought it would only be a matter of time before one of them recognized Asghar, stopped the car, and pulled all of us out onto the street. I imagined both of us standing beneath a crane, staring up at a noose. I tried not to let myself think about what they would do to Roksana.

We drove to a large house on the outskirts of the city where we were welcomed inside by a man whose accent told me he was from Azerbaijan. He was as old as my dad and stared at Roksana and me before taking Asghar off into another room. I didn't like him.

We were given a room with a thin foam mattress and little else. Later that night the man—who, though he told me his name, I always thought of as the Smuggler—came into the room, pulled out a map of Iran, and lay it on the floor. He plopped his fat finger down on Tehran and checked that we were both paying attention. First he would drive us northeast to the city of Tabriz. From there we'd take a bus to the town of Maku, right on the border with Turkey. "From there," he said, skipping his fingers across the border, "Turkey. Easy!"

"How do we get across the mountains?" Asghar asked.

"Bus. Very easy. Only a few hours. No problem at all."

I liked him less after this conversation. I wanted to believe him, but if it was so easy why did it cost so much?

The Smuggler asked Asghar where the money was, and he told him that his mother—who had driven back to her home in Shiraz after we arrived in Tehran—was going to bring it up in a couple of days. Again, it all sounded too easy, and when she finally did arrive (bringing Asghar's eighteen-year-old cousin, Firouz, with her too), there was a long and noisy argument between her and Asghar about how much she was having to pay to get both Roksana and me out in addition to her son. I had long since given up trying to change her opinion on anything, so I just sat quietly with Roksana as we tried to make ourselves invisible.

Ziynab eventually returned to Shiraz, but Firouz stayed with us when we left Tehran. Apparently he was coming with us to Turkey, though nobody had told me about this change in plans.

The drive to Tabriz in the Smuggler's cigarette-stained, beat-up car was uncomfortable. It wasn't just the tobacco stench or the failing suspension that bothered me but the conservative Islamic clothes I was wearing. We were heading toward one of Iran's most religious regions, one that was also well known as a route for smuggling everything from weapons to alcohol, people to drugs. The only protection I would have would be a heavy, black chador, a tight-fitting hood that covered most of my face, and a pair of scratchy gloves.

At Tabriz the Smuggler parked near the bus station and gave us our final instructions. "Take the bus to Maku, and wait at the terminal when you arrive. A little boy will come and find you and bring you to my mother's house there." He reached into a bag behind his seat, pulling out three small books and handing them to me. "When you are on the bus, pretend you're devout and read these."

Ever since we had left Tehran, the scenery outside had been changing. The mountains had grown taller and the snow deeper. I stepped out of the car at the station and pulled Roksana in close. The air was colder than any I'd ever felt before, and the foot of snow on the ground was way more than any we had ever seen in Isfahan. For the first time that day, I was glad of the extra clothes.

Even before we sat down I knew that we did not belong on the bus. We looked and sounded nothing like the rest of the passengers. If anyone so much as looked down the aisle, they'd know that we were the ones who were trying to escape.

Four hours in to the trip, and the bus slowed and came to a complete stop. I looked up from the Qur'an that had been open on my lap beside Roksana-ever since we left Tabriz and saw precisely what I had feared: a line of cars waiting at a checkpoint swarming with soldiers.

Asghar grabbed Roksana and pretended to be a concerned father desperately trying to soothe his infant daughter to sleep. I stared again at the Qur'an and wished for a miracle.

I heard soldiers board the bus. As soon as I saw the military boots covered in mud and snow come to a halt beside me, I knew it was over. "Where are you from?" he asked.

"Isfahan."

"Why are you going to Maku?" I felt sick and could think of nothing to say. Everyone knew that the only reason outsiders went to Maku was to escape into Turkey. "We are going to visit an Imam." It was a terrible answer, and I waited for him to tell me to get off the bus. But no such order came. Instead he moved farther down.

When the bus finally cleared the checkpoint, the soldiers had taken three passengers off. I watched them as they stood on the road. They looked terrified.

The rest of our journey was quiet and uneventful. A little boy approached us at the bus stop and called us by name, and we followed him along several streets. Maku was even colder than Tabriz, and poorer too. There were no sidewalks and barely any traffic. He led us into a house that was darker, older, and damper than any I had been in. Inside, the Smuggler was waiting for us. He barely said a word to us. He just pointed us to our room and told us not to leave the house, make any noise, or remove the board that covered the window.

We met his mother when she opened the door, holding a bucket for us to use as a toilet. She said that she would bring some food later on as well, but by the time she did I was asleep.

The Smuggler visited early the next day. I asked if I could go for a walk, but he told me that it was too risky. "Someone will see you," he said. "And it's obvious you don't belong here."

And so that was it. There was no lock on the door, and we were allowed to walk about the house, but there was nothing to see—only brown, unpainted walls and grimy windows that looked out onto the backs and sides of another house.

The rest of the day crept by, the only distraction being the lamb and egg that his mother brought us late in the afternoon. When Roksana was awake I devoted myself to her, but when she slept all I could do was stare at the thin, threadbare carpet.

Iranians can tell a lot about a house by looking at the carpet. In the west it is the art on the walls that reveal a person's taste, but in Iran the best art is always right beneath your feet. The best carpets come from Isfahan; they are made with silk and can cost thousands of dollars. I remembered the carpet I had back at home, and the day that Daniel had peed on it.

The memory caused me physical pain, not just from the

sounds of his screams that I could hear again, but the fact that I missed my boy so much. I tried to remember the smell and the feel of his head as I held him close. I tried, but the memory was weak.

———

The Smuggler visited every day, but he never had much to say. Most of the time Asghar talked with him about the plans for our escape. I stayed silent throughout, and the waiting continued.

On the tenth day the Smuggler had some news for us. "We will leave tomorrow, but first you need some new shoes," he said, looking at my canvas sneakers.

"Why?" said Asghar.

"Because those shoes are no good for walking in the mountains."

Asghar's anger was quick, but I knew he was trying to control it. "Walking? You said we were going by bus."

The Smuggler just shrugged and pointed back at my shoes. "Like I said, those are no good, but I can buy you some walking boots. Give me some money, and I will do it today."

I didn't have any money, but Asghar appeared to be deaf to the conversation. The only thing I could do was hand over my gold necklace.

When he was gone Asghar and Firouz talked about the change in plan. Soon, though, they ran out of things to say. We all realized that we were powerless.

I started to worry about my clothes. I had not even brought a coat with me, just a light vest. If it was too snowy for sneakers it was sure to be too cold for anything else I had to wear. I wondered about asking the Smuggler to buy me something warm to wear, but I had nothing left to sell.

The evening we left, the Smuggler came with a couple of duffel bags and told us to swap them for our suitcases. He also gave us each a white sheet, but said nothing about why.

It was just barely still light as we walked to his car. A man I'd never seen before drove us down the warren of muddy roads, the headlights weak in the gloom. It was only when we pulled out onto a main road that I saw them: the mountains. They towered above us, patches of dark against the sky, like giant storm clouds that had been wrestled all the way to the ground.

The driver pointed the car out of the town, turned off his lights, and drove down an empty road that was lined with rocks. Soon the engine was straining as the car began the climb, and we quickly slowed to a halt. The road ahead of us ended in a pile of snow-capped boulders.

"Now we walk," said the Smuggler, opening his door and stamping his feet warm.

The mountains seemed even bigger now that we were among them, rising up above us like impregnable castle walls. I stared, searching for a path, but I could see nothing but rock, snow, and darkness.

"Where's the path?" asked Asghar as the car arced away from us and sank into the darkness.

The Smuggler waved his hand up at the sky. "Up there," he said. He pulled his own white sheet out of his bag and arranged it over his head. His eyes peered out through specially cut holes, making him look like he was dressing up as a ghost to scare some children. "Put yours on," he said, "and follow me." He turned from us and took a step. His leg plunged knee-deep into the snow.

I FELT EVERY BIT LIKE THE GHOST THAT
I must have looked like. The mountain boots that had cost me
my gold necklace were already soaked through, and every step
was a battle of strength and concentration. I had already run out
of both. I was exhausted and cold in a way I had never known
before. I had nothing left within me.

We had been walking less than an hour.

Right from the start we moved in silence, our bodies swaying from side to side as we planted each foot in the snow. I had
Roksana in my arms and had to take extra care, which meant I
fell back behind the others. Asghar would stop and wait until
I caught up, then haul me by the shoulder for a while, but in a
few minutes I'd be at the back again, watching the three swaying
white sheets disappear into the darkness ahead.

The ground soon changed. The deep snow remained, but the
ascent became so steep that it was impossible not to use your
hands. Asghar took Roksana and carried her in one of the duffel bags, the zipper open just enough to make sure she got air. I
scrambled and shivered behind as best I could, my numb fingers
groping for safety among the sharp rocks.

All the time we wore our sheets. Seeing the world through two
tiny holes, hearing nothing but the sound of my own breathing,

feeling nothing but the pain in my limbs and the warmth of my breath. It turned my thoughts inward. It was not long before I was wondering how long the journey would take and fearing how long I would be able to last.

There was only one positive that I could hold onto—that Roksana had so far remained asleep. As long as she was not distressed, I knew that I would be able to keep going.

I don't know how many hours we walked at first, but at one point I looked up and saw that the Smuggler had stopped near a herd of goats. We waited at a distance and looked on as he went and spoke with the shepherd boy up ahead.

The Smuggler returned with old cheese and bread, both of them so hard and dry they had lost all taste. Not that it mattered. I ate in silence while Roksana stirred in my arms and drank from the bottle of milk I had brought with me.

I put Roksana back in her bag and looked at my shoes. My feet were so numb that I'd been hitting my shoes on rocks all the way up. The soles were falling off both of them. I ripped in half one of my chadors and wrapped it around my feet, hoping to hold the shoes together for a while more. As I finished, it was time to move on. It was almost a relief to get up and walk again, for in the few minutes that we had stopped I had felt my body temperature drop. With no gloves and no warm clothes, just jeans and my light jacket, the only hope I had of keeping warm was to keep moving.

Between the moon and the snow, we were able to see the ground in front of us, though whenever we approached the top of a peak, it was hard to tell where the mountains stopped and the darkness began. Our route had us scrambling up the rock face on all fours one moment, then sliding down over loose rocks the next. Apart from the snow tracks we left ourselves there didn't seem to be any real path that we were following. It was impossible to know how far we had come or how much farther there was to go. Everywhere looked the same, and once we had left the farmer's hut behind, we'd seen no more sign of life at all. The longer we walked, the less I thought about how soon we'd be arriving in Turkey, and the more I thought about how I could survive long enough to make it.

As the sun rose behind us, the Smuggler led us into a gap in the mountain. "We will sleep here," he said, throwing his bag down. "When it's night, we'll walk again."

Though the sun rose and the air grew warmer, the fact that we were motionless allowed the cold to bite even deeper than it had the night before. The pain was deeper, as if every bone was ice and every finger was fire. The Smuggler slept, wrapped in his hat and gloves, his thick jacket and sweater, but I was too cold to sleep. Even wearing every item of clothing that I had brought with me didn't help. All I could do was close my eyes, pull my knees in close, and rock from side to side.

———

Soon after it fell dark and we started walking, Roksana began to cry. She had spent much of the day either asleep or feeding, but now, as we trekked our way through the mountains, it was getting harder to pacify her.

After a few hours we stopped at another wooden shack, where we boiled snow and made up some more bottles with our powdered milk. Roksana settled a little, finally going back to sleep. With some more cheese and bread inside us, we pushed on.

When she started crying again, Roksana was louder than

ever. Her cries echoed off the mountainside, and the Smuggler made us all stop. "Make her quiet," he hissed, his face inches from mine. "She'll get us caught out here."

The best I could do as we stood there was hold her close and muffle the worst of her screams. But she was frozen, and nothing I could do would stop her. The Smuggler told us to start walking again, and before we started clambering over loose rocks and up steep slopes again, Asghar took her and put her back in the bag. Somehow she quieted a little. Slowly, inch by inch, we pressed on.

It had become impossible to concentrate. My mind drifted like the snow that was blowing about the mountains. I thought about Daniel and remembered the sight of him waving outside my parents' house as we drove away. I remembered Mohammad shouting about Khomeini into the dark night. I saw my father smoking his hookah, laughing as the dancing turned wild around him. And I remembered how loud I cried as I listened to the poppy song months after Mohammad died. Was this the future I was facing? *When you die, I die, so very soon.*

The sound of Roksana's crying brought me back. We had stopped, and Asghar had placed Roksana in her bag on a low rock. He was helping Firouz bandage up his shoes. The Smuggler, meanwhile, was standing over Roksana, reaching for the handle of the duffel, then turning away and walking down behind a rock. He disappeared, and with him Roksana's voice grew fainter.

I sprang to life. "Stop him, Asghar!" I shouted, running over to the rock. Beneath was a steep slope, and though I could not see the bottom, I could hear Roksana's cries coming from below. I jumped forward, my legs keeping my balance for the first two strides, but soon giving way. I slipped and scraped down through the snow toward the figure I could see below.

"Give me back my daughter!" I shouted as I reached the Smuggler. He was standing over the bag, his back to me. He turned. In his hand was a gun.

"I'm going to kill her," he said as Asghar and Firouz joined me. "It'll be easier for all of us if I do."

"No!" Asghar and I both said at once. "We'll keep her quiet," I begged. "She won't make any noise, I promise. Please, just give me back my daughter."

He waved the pistol back toward Roksana, who was still crying in the bag. "You can't promise that. You can't keep her quiet out here." He paused. He reached into his pocket and pulled out what looked like a bottle. "I'll let her live if you let me keep her asleep."

After a while—and two capfuls of the Smuggler's medicine—Roksana's crying calmed. Soon she was asleep, and our journey continued.

———

We spent the next day in another cave. It was colder this time, and the bottles of milk we brought with us had all frozen. Though we tried to thaw them out by placing them next to our bodies, it was impossible to melt enough to satisfy Roksana. She had no choice but to go without once again.

We walked through the third night, rested again the next day, and then walked through the fourth. At first I was always the quickest to reach Roksana whenever she awoke, but soon the cold and the exhaustion overtook me, slowing me down, dulling my senses. Whenever she stirred, the Smuggler was there, tipping cap after cap of the thick, smoky liquid into her mouth.

All I could do was watch through the two tiny holes in my sheet. None of it felt real.

We only stopped for a short time on the fifth day. At least, that's how it seemed to me. I was glad at least that my toes and fingers had stopped hurting, but when I looked at them, both my hands and feet were black. The skin peeled off like it was wet paper.

We were soon moving again, but by now my legs had failed. I lay on the ground to rest, and Asghar grabbed the neck of my jacket and hauled me over the snow. I remember thinking how odd it was that I was colder than I'd ever been, yet I didn't feel scared. Death was close. I could feel it.

The Smuggler stopped us at the top of a steep slope that led a long way down. "You two go that way," he said to Asghar and me. "I have to take Firouz another way."

"Why?" I heard Asghar say.

The Smuggler said something about us being in Turkey already and how we needed to split up to avoid getting caught by their border guards, but I was drifting again. I was grateful that I was finally still. All I wanted to do was sleep.

———

I felt the earth start to move beneath me. I was falling, slowly at first, then quicker. I was out of control. My neck hurt, and so did my back. Somewhere nearby, I could hear Asghar cursing. I knew what this meant—that any second now he would hurt me with his fists—but I didn't care so much.

"He took the bag," Asghar said, his face suddenly appearing large and loud in front of me. "The bag with the money, the papers, the jewelry. It's all gone."

I sat up. We were at the bottom of a hollow, a small valley fenced in by steep sides. "Where are we?"

"He tricked us. He said there was a road down here, but there's nothing."

Asghar went and tried to scramble up one side of the valley, like a spider trapped in a jar.

I wanted to check on Roksana and pulled myself over to where the bag was.

The zipper was half open.

Her skin was white, as white as the snow. But it was mottled too, strange patterns inked beneath her skin. I put my cheek to her mouth, but the air was cold. I felt her chest but there was no movement. I picked her up. So thin. So light.

I fell back on the rocks, her body held to mine. There was nothing to her. No breath. No heat. No life.

I opened my mouth and screamed.

Asghar came and picked her up. He sobbed into her chest, the thick bundle of clothes swallowing his cries.

But it was getting dark, and we had to move quickly if we were to find the materials we needed to build a fire and keep warm. He lay Roksana's body beside me, gathered some sticks, and made a fire. "It doesn't matter anymore," he said, as the little tower struggled to catch light. He blew and blew, sending great clouds of smoke into the air.

Then I saw them. Asghar was still kneeling, blowing and blowing, and as the flames wrapped around the wood, I saw their eyes reflected in the light. I whispered to Asghar, and he stopped and stared.

"Wolves," he said. "They can smell her."

He got up and gathered stones, building first a base, then a small wall around the base. I protested when he took Roksana and placed her in the middle. He was building our daughter a grave. "They'll eat her otherwise," he said. I let go then.

When the pile of rocks was complete, Asghar left. He was convinced there was a road nearby and wanted to find it.

All I wanted to do was join my daughter.

I tore at the rocks that covered her with the palms of my hands, my fingers no longer good for anything. I pulled her out and held Roksana to me.

I wanted to end it all. I rocked back and forth, howling from deep inside.

I swung my head down upon the rocks with all the force that I could manage. A pain sharper than any Asghar had ever given me tore through my head, but still it was not enough. I could feel it, and I wanted to feel nothing.

I hit my head on the rocks again, and again, wishing the end would come.

When I could hit no more, I opened my lungs and shouted at God. "Where are you?" I knew he could not hear me, or if he could that he would not answer, but I called to him all the same. I only had one request of him—that he would end my suffering and take my life. That was all I wanted. Nothing more.

I listened to the words echoing all around me. "Where are you?" I shouted again. Nothing but my own voice came back to me.

I lay down.

The wolves could have us both soon enough.

I FOUND A ROAD! WE'VE GOT A WAY OUT!"

I turned away from Asghar's voice. It was dark, the fire had gone out, and the cold was deeper inside me than it had been at any point in the journey. But it seemed the wolves had left us behind.

"Come on, Annahita, we've made it! I can pull you up. Let me take Roksana, and we'll get out."

"You go without me," I said. "Leave us here."

When he spoke again, there was something different about his voice. Instead of his usual anger and hatred, he was softer, quieter. "Please," he said. "Let's take her somewhere we can bury her properly."

I could just about stand, but my legs and hands were too weak to climb up out of the valley. Asghar found a long stick, which I held onto, and he dragged me up and onto the plateau beyond.

We walked until we heard dogs barking. I looked up and saw their black fur standing out against the snow. "Sit down!" Asghar shouted to me as he sat and put his hands on top of his head. "Put your hands like this, or they'll attack."

The two dogs were soon upon us, barking with spit flying and teeth bared. Behind them, two figures emerged—soldiers in white winter uniforms. They talked at us, rather than shouted. I knew enough Turkish to recognize the language but not enough to know what they were saying. They helped us up and had us follow them back the way they had come.

We dropped down from the plateau and joined a track that led us to another hollow, like the one we'd just come from. Only, this time, there was a fire that sent flames as tall as a man into the darkness. We sat close to the fire, Roksana in the bag between us.

I could see the soldiers better in the firelight. One was a boy no older than myself; the other was old. Neither of them seemed to know what to say to us, and the boy smiled awkwardly as the older man spoke into his radio.

Asghar was tense beside me. "What's wrong?" I said.

"Maybe they're not Turkish. Maybe they're from Azerbaijan." It was possible, after all. The language was similar, but the politics of Azerbaijan were different than Turkey's. If the soldiers really were who Asghar suspected they were, we'd be sent back to Iran straight away.

The old soldier finished with the radio and walked over to us. He looked at us carefully before turning his eyes to the bags. Dropping his rifle from his shoulder, he went to prod Roksana's bag with the end of his bayonet.

I shouted at him to stop and threw myself across the bag. Carefully I undid the zipper to show them her body.

Two eyes stared back at me.

Her skin was still white, but her eyes were wide open. She was breathing again, straining her head this way and that in search of food. I couldn't understand it. I had been sure that she was dead, that it was over. There had been no breath, no sound, and no sign of movement from her when we were up on the mountain. But now, here she was—alive again.

My cries were incomprehensible to the soldiers. "Bebek! Bebek!" they said. "It's just a baby!"

I held onto her, sobbing. I was so happy that we hadn't left her under the rocks, so happy that Asghar had brought us both out from our open grave. I was so happy that she was back. All the pain I was feeling—from where I had hit my head, from the frostbite on my feet and hands, from the exhaustion and the cold—it all disappeared in an instant.

I paid no attention to Asghar or the soldiers anymore. Roksana was alive. That was everything.

I barely noticed when two jeeps arrived. Roksana and I climbed into one, while Asghar was taken away in another. I only glanced about me as we moved farther and farther down the mountain, finally coming to stop at a cave that went back deep into the mountainside. I saw the soldiers moving around and took the place against the wall that they showed me.

The sun could have fallen from the sky, and I would have paid it no attention. All that mattered were the two dark eyes staring back at me from the bundle of blankets that I clasped to my chest.

It felt like hours passed while I crouched there and whispered my love to my baby. I could not begin to understand what had happened to her; all I could do was replay in my mind the moment when I opened the bag and saw her looking back at me—alive after I had been so convinced that she was dead. I cried constant tears of gratitude, though who I was thanking I did not know. Was it God? Had he forgiven me my rages against him? It did not seem likely, but who else could be behind such a miracle?

When I finally did look up and out of the cave, the sun had long since faded and a pale moon had climbed into the clear sky. I wasn't as cold this far down the mountain, and a fire gave extra warmth.

I heard feet approach and looked up to see a soldier not much older than Asghar walk toward me with a bucket. He put it down at my feet and gestured to Roksana. I could not understand what he was saying. I panicked, pushing myself back against the wall, pulling Roksana even tighter. The soldier spread his hands and gestured to Roksana. "Wash?" he said slowly. "Wash baby."

I stared as he retreated, tracing every step until he disappeared into one of the buildings on the other side of the yard. The bucket was half full of warm water, but before I could do much more than contemplate washing her and cleaning her diaper, the sound of more footsteps broke the silence.

The soldier was back, but this time he was struggling to keep up with an older officer speeding toward me. Before I had time to get up and run he was in front of me, crouching down, his eyes wide and smile broad as he peered in at Roksana. As he carefully edged back the blankets I saw his hands were creased and cracked.

"She is beautiful," he said in near perfect Farsi. I pulled Roksana back toward me, burrowing her deeper down within the blankets. He pulled his hands back and looked at me. "Are you hungry?"

I didn't know how long it had been since I had eaten. We had run out of food long before Roksana started crying. It felt like a whole year had passed since we met the last farmer and ate the bread and cheese he had sold us. The thought of food sent a painful wave of hunger through me. I studied the officer's face. "Yes," I said eventually, nodding.

"Then come with me," he said as he stood. "My wife will take care of you and the baby." I followed behind him and the young soldier, across the cave, and toward a waiting car. My legs burned as I walked, my muscles screaming their protest with each step.

The officer was as good as his word, and his wife was every bit as kind as I could have hoped. He and the young soldier soon left us with her, and she fussed around just like my own mother did whenever she encountered a newborn baby. She spoke no Farsi at all, which suited me fine. I was happy just to sit somewhere safe and warm and watch as she took occasional peeks at Roksana.

Then the officer's wife turned her attention to me, bringing out hot, sweet tea and fruit. The taste was better than anything I could remember, and the feeling of being full again reminded me of home. Though the room was small, dark, and barely furnished apart from some low chairs and a heater in the corner, my mind took me back to the summer days in Isfahan. I could close my eyes and be back in the bright main room at home. It was easy to recall what it felt like to be surrounded by people and laughter and never-ending feasts spread out across the floor as we sat around the edge of the room on brightly colored cushions.

I pictured Daniel running after his cousins, trying to keep up with longer legs and stronger lungs. I remembered what it felt like to crouch next to him in front of a cake with two candles. The way his eyes grew wide with the flames. How the soft heat on our faces and the rhythm of his breathing next to me seemed perfectly matched.

It hurt to think of these times. They felt too distant, too far back in the past and too many mountains away from me. I had left everything behind—my home, my family, my son—in the hopes of safety, in search of refuge. Would I ever find a home again? Would I ever see my son?

When Roksana drifted off to sleep the woman urged me to place her between two cushions and go with her through a curtain at the back of the room. She showed me to a washbowl and a mirror, motioning for me to look at myself.

I did not recognize the face that I saw.

It belonged to someone far older than me. To someone who had never smiled but only ever cried. To someone who looked as though she had been eating nothing but dirt and coal for months.

I tried to wash away some of the dried mud from my lips. Nothing came off. As I examined my hands I saw it was spread across my fingertips too—patches of black surrounded by open, bloody sores. I looked closer at my face. It was not mud, but frostbite.

For two days Roksana and I stayed in the officer's house. His wife cared for us, feeding me hot soup and constantly bringing warm water for me to bathe with when I was awake, leaving me to sleep for hours and hours at a time with Roksana curled up in my arms. She was a newborn again, sleepy and content just like she had been a month earlier back in Iran. I needed to recover too, to let my body begin to heal from the ordeal it had just been through.

The officer came and went, and we spoke little. Whenever I asked him about where Asghar had gone or when he was coming back he just tutted and told me to rest some more and that he would tell me soon enough.

Early on the third day I woke up to see him standing over me. "You can see your husband now," he said. "Come with me."

I followed him out of his home, Roksana in my arms and her

bag—heavy with almonds, dates, and cheese that the wife had given me—dragging at my side.

Asghar was waiting by a police car. He looked tired, but nothing worse.

Before we could talk much we were put in the car and driven off. Two soldiers I did not recognize were in the front, and while I assumed that Asghar and I were free to talk, his fixed stare and tense body told me that it would be better if I kept quiet.

It did not take more than an hour to reach our destination—a large police station. It took less than a minute to understand that we were no longer to be treated as guests. As we were ordered out of the car and through the metal gates that were shut quickly behind us, it was clear we were now prisoners.

Asghar was taken away by two soldiers. A boy barely old enough to shave took Roksana and me to a cell on our own, locking the bars behind us without saying a word. There was no water, no heat, and no bed. Just a rough blanket on the asphalt floor, a rusted bucket that smelled like a sewer, and a cracked and barred window set high in the wall.

I tried to listen for clues that might tell me what was going on. There was nothing to hear. I tried looking out of the window, but there was nothing but sky to see. Roksana slept for a while but soon grew hungry. I only had a little milk for her, and once it was gone her cries returned. The more I tried and failed to feed her the more upset she became. She cried so loud that I started to fear that a soldier would come in and threaten to kill her. When I closed my eyes all I could see was the Smuggler with his gun in one hand and Roksana's bag in the other. I begged her to be quiet, pleading with her with all my strength.

When the door finally opened, I scurried to a corner, trying to hide Roksana from view. I needn't have worried, for it was the boy soldier again. In one hand he held out a small packet, in another a drinking canteen and bucket of water. He placed them by the door and left.

I added the sugar to the water and hoped that it would be enough to keep her going. She cried some, slept some, and I did my best to keep her happy and clean. There were times when she curled into me and I would kiss the soft skin on her head and cheeks and forget all about where we were or what had happened. But for every one of those moments there were many more where I feared what would happen when the door next opened. We were like winter leaves in the wind: without power, without strength. Just waiting for the moment when we would be thrown out of the eye of the storm.

I was taken for questioning more than once. They spoke good Farsi and always wanted to know the same things: Where was I from? Why was I in Turkey? Why had we come the way we did? Why did we leave? What was happening with the regime in Iran?

Whenever they asked about Asghar, it was clear to me that they thought he was a big deal. They asked what I knew about his military career. I told them the minimum that I could: that he worked in Isfahan and that he never told me anything about his work. In truth, I knew a little more, like the fact that he was an officer working with technical systems and that he probably had valuable information that they would want. But that was his story to tell, not mine.

And so they would return me to my cell, letting me out

occasionally to use the bathroom. I was trying to wash out Roksana's diaper in the bathroom sink one morning, when a woman greeted me in Farsi.

"Where are you from?" she said, quietly.

I told her, and she asked where I was going next.

"I don't know." I shrugged. "Do you?"

She smiled weakly. "They're sending us back home to Tehran."

I tried to imagine what returning home would be like. I felt the joy of seeing Daniel as well as the fear of the Sepah. "If you can, would you phone my parents and tell them I'm okay?"

She nodded and smiled, and I wrote the number down for her before a guard came in and split us up. I had no idea whether she would remember, or even whether she would be allowed her freedom once she returned, but the thought of Daniel and my parents getting the message warmed me deep inside.

—

"You're done," said an officer later that morning as he stood in front of my cell. "You can leave now." I gathered Roksana and my bag—now almost empty of the food that I had been given—and followed him out to a waiting car. Asghar was already inside, and the engine was running.

"Where are we going?" he asked as I got in.

"We're taking you to a hotel," the officer said as he shut the door behind me.

The driver laughed and pulled onto the road.

FROM THE OUTSIDE IT LOOKED LIKE A
hospital from another lifetime. Tall walls and smeared windows
stared down as we drove in through the gates. Inside it looked
like a school that had long since been abandoned. Long corridors
were punctuated with identical doors, all of them scratched and
stained. All of them closed.

Apart from the guard who led us, we didn't see a single person as we walked along behind him. The place looked empty, but
it did not feel that way. Behind the doors and around the cor-
ners there were the faintest noises of people moving. We were not
alone, but we had no idea who else was hidden within these walls.

We walked up a narrow stairwell and out onto the fourth
floor. The guard walked us to the far end of the corridor in
silence, unlocked the door, and waved us inside.

He locked the door behind us, and Asghar and I looked
about. It was a big room, and each of the windows were painted
over in white paint that almost smothered the daylight outside.
Between the dim bulb overhead and the little light that leaked in
where the paint had grown thin, we could see enough to know
what secrets the room held.

One corner had two metal cages, divided down the middle by a
wall. Each cage was small, only just big enough for a man to crouch

in or sit with legs hunched up close to his chest. The rest of the room was empty, apart from a single wooden bed, its foam mattress hanging down through the gaps in the metal wire that was trying to hold the frame together. When I touched the mattress my fingers came away damp and smelling of vomit and urine.

But it was the room's last bit of furniture that really worried me. A large table stood in the middle, its wooden top covered in deep scratches and dark stains. Scattered around the floor like bird feed in a city park were dozens of bloody fingernails and broken wooden sticks.

Every wall had blood on it.

"I'm scared, Asghar. What will they do to us?"

He walked over to the window and tried to scratch off some paint. He pulled his hands back quickly when we heard the lock turning and a man and a woman walked in. Asghar was soon taken out, while the woman remained. "Your pockets," she said, motioning to me to empty them onto the table.

She said nothing as she poked among the handful of items I still possessed. There were a few coins, some nail clippers, none of it either valuable or dangerous. "Your clothes too," she said, casually. I hesitated, but she looked up, staring hard at me.

When she had finished patting me down and was finally satisfied that I was not hiding anything, she had me take Roksana out of the bag where I had placed her, searching through it as though it contained some hidden secrets. The bag that had carried her over the mountains, that I had been convinced was her coffin, was now her crib. Besides a blanket and a few outfits for Roksana and myself, the bag was all the lady let me keep.

In return she gave me an empty bottle and took me out of the room and back down to the end of the corridor. She wanted to show me where the bathroom was and demonstrate how I could collect water and wash Roksana's diaper. There were three toilet booths, two with closed doors. She saw me looking at them. "Only this one," she said, pointing to the third. "Never those."

―――

Asghar and I were sitting on the floor by the bed when the door opened again. What little light the painted windows let in had long since disappeared, and I was drifting in and out of sleep. The noise of the lock was enough to shock me awake.

Two men with rifles walked in and marched us back down to the courtyard in silence. A jeep was waiting, its engine running. I couldn't see inside; every window was covered in cloth.

One of the guards pointed at Roksana and jerked his head at Asghar. I handed her over, and someone immediately put a thick, dark bag on my head. My hands were pulled behind my back and handcuffed before I was pressed into the jeep.

I could feel one of the guards getting in next to me, his hips pushing me over toward the door, his shoulder pinning me back against my seat. Asghar complained loudly about his bag from the other side. I could hear Roksana stirring in his arms, protesting that she had been taken away from me. I wanted to call out to her, to let my voice try to soothe her a little, but between the stench of the bag and the pressure of the guard next to me, my voice choked. I willed myself to breathe, to stay calm and not to think about what might happen next.

The first moment I felt hands touching me I tried to jerk my body to the side and get out of the way. But I was already pressed up against the door and had nowhere to go. The hands wouldn't stop. They carried on, touching me wherever they wanted. I had no idea who they belonged to, but I knew I couldn't tell them to stop. If I did protest, who knows what they would do to Roksana? All I could do was wait, to cry in the darkness and wish the drive would end soon.

———

The jeep finally stopped, and the hands retreated. Once we were out in the air again my hands were freed and Roksana was placed back in my arms. The bag, however, remained on. I tried to keep my footing as Roksana and I were led away, beneath the orange glow of lights and into a building that was full of heavy, metal doors.

When the bag was finally removed I was expecting metal bars and concrete walls, but instead I saw a room lined with sheets of wood. It was like an oversized box, a scaled-up doll's house with one light and one table with two chairs on either side of it. Even the door was strange; there was just a faint crack of a door-shaped outline and no handle anywhere to be seen.

Roksana didn't care about any of it. Ever since we had come down from the mountains she had only ever wanted to be in my arms. She would sleep soundly for hours with her head pushed up against the crook of my elbow, her legs across my waist.

We were in the strange wooden room alone, and as the time passed—maybe one hour, maybe two—the feelings of panic and fear eased a little. But the moment I heard the door open behind me, our captors returned in full.

The man who stood in the doorway was unlike any of the officers, guards, or soldiers I had met since arriving in Turkey.

He wore no uniform, yet it was obvious he was in charge as he turned back, whispered something to a young officer behind him, and strolled into the room. He sat opposite me, spread his hands on the table between us, and looked me up and down.

Every other officer I had spoken to so far had almost seemed bored by Roksana and me, as if we were of no consequence or threat. But the man now opposite didn't just look at me, he studied me. I wanted to pull my chador over both Roksana and me and hide.

He waited the longest time before speaking. His voice was low and I couldn't place the accent, but his Farsi was perfect.

"You're a mystery," he said, smiling. "But we'll work that out eventually. All you need to know now is that my name is Beautiful Hands." He smirked, and my eyes followed his down. I'd not looked at his hands the whole time he'd been sitting there, but as I did I saw that the name was ironic. From the edge of his shirt to the tips of his fingers, his skin was mottled brown and white, like a diseased plant.

I looked up. He was staring at me. No smiles this time. Just a look that went deep inside me.

"How many guns does Iran have?"

"I'm sorry?"

Slower this time, like he was talking to a child. "How. Many. Guns. Does. Iran. Have?"

"I don't know," I said, shrugging.

He tapped his fingers a little. "How many army bases?"

"I don't know."

More tapping. "Okay, then. Who are the key people right now?"

"I don't know. I'm sorry, but I don't know anything about this."

He held the silence for a moment, then burst out laughing. "I don't know, I don't know, I don't know!" he chanted, mocking my voice and pulling strange faces. The laughter soon snapped shut, and the silence returned. He pushed his chair back, stood up, and put his hands in his pockets. "You'll have to do better than that."

I didn't see him again that night, but Roksana and I were not alone in the room. As soon as Beautiful Hands left, an officer came in and stood by the door. He said nothing at all, but whenever I felt sleep take hold of me, he would kick my chair or prod my shoulder with the stock of his rifle.

When I asked to go to the bathroom, I was bagged again and led out, the officer's hand gripping tight the top of my arm. I stayed in the cubicle as long as I could, leaning against the wall, my body giving into sleep like a stone plunging to the bottom of a deep pool. When the shouting and knocking on the door woke me up, I'd never felt so nauseated and dizzy.

———

There was just enough light to know that it was daytime when they bagged me again and pushed me into the car. I could not tell whether it was the same guard sitting beside me, but on the drive back to the place they called the Hotel, the hands returned. Though I was desperately tired, the fear kept me awake.

Back in our room with the single bed and the bloody fingernails, I put a blanket on the floor and held Roksana to my chest. The floor was cold and hard, but it was better than lying on the filthy mattress or the broken bed frame. Asghar, Roksana, and I spent the rest of the day asleep.

The door opened once to bring us each a tray of rice and beans, and again whenever we banged on it asking to be taken to the bathroom. Apart from this, we were left alone, living like nocturnal creatures. I tried to forget about the previous night, but as the faint light from the windows grew fainter still, I started to hope desperately that we would be left alone.

Only when it was dark did the two guards return with their rifles and black sacks. They took us down to the waiting jeep. When I felt my shoulders pushed back and my hips squashed against the door, I knew that every part of the previous night's events were about to repeat.

Beautiful Hands was the same as the night before, only this time there were far more questions. How many military bases were there on the borders between Turkey and Iran? What was the size of the army? Where were the main training sites? How many troops were in Azerbaijan? I didn't know the answers to any of his questions, and again he ridiculed me. Maybe he thought I would break if he humiliated me enough, but after two years of life with Asghar, I was used to it.

What frightened me was the knowledge that there were terrible things happening behind other closed doors nearby. The bloody fingernails at the Hotel told me what that room had been used for in the past, but as I sat in the wooden room I often heard men crying out in agony, screaming in terror before being swallowed in silence.

As the days passed and the nighttime questioning continued, I began to grow more and more worried that it would be my turn soon. If they believed I really did know something about Iran's military, how much longer would their patience last? When would they finally decide that the only way to get the truth out of me would be through violence?

That sense of worry turned into outright panic the day I was left alone in the bathroom at the Hotel. It was early one morning, and I had left Roksana with Asghar as I went to collect water and wash her diaper. The officer who had escorted me looked tired and bored, and as the bathroom door closed behind me I heard his footsteps drift down the hall.

I had only ever used the one cubicle that was unlocked, and I hadn't given the other two much thought. But as I washed my hands that morning I heard a voice calling out. "Khahar!" it said quietly in my own language. "Sister!"

I edged over. "Who are you?"

"A boy. I'm twelve years old and I—"

The bathroom door crashed open behind me. "Why you talking?" the soldier yelled at me. I tried to back away, to say that it was a mistake. He blocked my way out, then seemed to think for a moment.

"You want to look inside?" he sneered. "Okay, then."

He pulled out a thick bunch of keys and unlocked the cubicle door. As soon as the lock clicked the door sprung open toward us. Two bodies—one a child's, another a man's—spilled out and lay in a pile at our feet. I could not tell whether both were alive at first, but as the guard started to hit them with his rifle they both groaned and flinched away from the blows.

The cubicle had been divided down the middle by a large sheet of wood. The spaces on either side were so small that no one could have lay or even sat down inside them.

After a few more hits the guard lifted each back up to their feet and forced them back inside. They stood like broken mario-nettes as he swung the door shut and locked it.

"You don't talk again like that," he said. "Ever."

Day after day we stayed in the room with the bloody fingernails on the fourth floor. Every night and every day followed the same routine of blindfolds and jeep rides, endless questions, and the torment of being made to stay awake. In the moments when I was able to sleep my dreams were dominated by the fear of Beautiful Hands tearing Roksana from my arms and locking me inside the third cubicle.

One night, as the second week ended, Beautiful Hands told me he had a surprise in store. "You're not going back to the Hotel this morning."

I knew better than to give him the satisfaction of asking where we were going, but I couldn't resist.

"Ah!" he said, a broad grin stuck on his face. "That would be telling, wouldn't it?"

Beneath my hood I could smell the damp air, hear the muffled shouts and cries in the distance. I heard Asghar sit next to me, and he passed me Roksana. I feared that this was the moment things would get even worse.

When the blindfold came off we were sitting in a corridor. The walls were darker than any of the others I'd seen, and the lights lower. I couldn't imagine anything good could happen in such a place.

A guard arrived, escorting someone else whose face was hidden behind a blindfold. The guard forced him to sit, then pulled off the bag.

"Firouz?" Asghar and I said in surprise.

It was him, and once the guard left us we were able to talk in whispers for a while. I hadn't seen him since the mountains. He looked ill and tired.

By instinct we all fell silent when we heard the guard return. He took Roksana from me and passed her back to Asghar. Then he pulled me up by the arms and led me to a metal door. I was relieved to see that there was a standard-sized interview room beyond it—not a cupboard in which I would be forced to stand.

I sat on a chair and waited.

When Beautiful Hands came in and started talking he seemed almost bored. He asked the strangest questions, like what my name was, where I was from, what Asghar's name was. Within ten minutes he knocked on the door and had me taken out to another identical room. Someone brought Roksana to me, then left and locked me in.

It took an hour or maybe more until the door opened again. When it did the guard pulled me out and led me back to where Asghar and Firouz we sitting. Both of their faces were swollen messes of blood and bruising. Firouz refused to look at me. Asghar's stare was full of the same menace that I remembered from back in Isfahan. In the month since we had left, he had not laid a finger on me. Not that he had been kind or loving, but the violence had disappeared. For good? That's what I hoped. But as he now glared at me, I knew I had been naive to wish such a thing.

"I will deal with you," he said.

———

Back at the Hotel, the violence returned. It was not the worst beating Asghar had ever given me, but the pain it inflicted stung deep inside. His fists seemed to have a new weight to them. My bones felt brittle, and my skin felt like a thin layer of ice.

It was only when he had finished that he spoke.

"Why did you tell him everything?"

"To Beautiful Hands? I didn't say anything to him at all. All he did was ask me my name and things like that."

Another slap sent a fresh wave of pain into my cheek. "You're lying, you whore. He told me that you'd told him everything."

"I didn't," I begged. "He lied."

Asghar paused. I knew he believed me. But it didn't stop him grabbing me by the hair and hitting me once more.

I LAY ON THE BUNK, HIDING DEEP IN the darkness. I was listening to the sound of my husband getting drunk with the guard in the room above our cell. I took the smallest sips of breath that I could. I had to be able to hear everything that was going on.

Roksana was asleep on my chest. There was no chance of sleep for me. I could feel my heart in my throat and the adrenaline in my guts. I needed to be alert to every sound that dropped down from above. Every clink of every bottle, every drunken shout of laughter, every set of footsteps as they slumped across the boards above me. Soon enough, Asghar would pass out. That's when the guard would come down to the basement and try to rape me.

It was not the first time, and I guessed it would not be the last.

Two weeks had passed since Beautiful Hands had beaten Asghar and Firouz. I heard that Firouz had been sent back to Iran, but when Asghar and I returned to the Hotel that afternoon—and after he had given me my share of the beatings—we had been taken from the fourth floor and shown to a new cell in the basement.

I was nervous when the guards first took us down the stone

steps. It looked like a fairy-tale dungeon, with its dark walls, weak lights, and rusted bars that stood floor to ceiling across the front of each of five cells, each one full of men. By the look of them, nearly all of the inmates were from Iran, Pakistan, or Afghanistan.

I could feel them staring as I walked. I tried not to look, but it was impossible not to notice the way some rubbed their eyes and gazed over at Roksana and me. I hated it. Anywhere would be better than this. Even a room with bloodied fingernails and broken sticks on the floor.

I tried to calm myself, looking for something that would hold back the fear. At least there was more than one bunk. At least there were mattresses. At least the other three men in our cell looked old and weak.

As soon as they saw me they started to complain. They told the guards it was humiliating to have to share with a woman. The guards just shrugged, pulled them out, and bundled them into one of the other cells.

I looked closer at the mattresses. Each of them stained with blood, urine, and feces. The light was dim, but bright enough to reveal a floor so filthy that I sat quickly on a mattress and decided there and then never to let Roksana get down.

Roksana was already crying. "Make the baby shut up," said the guard in the cell with us. I held her close and bounced her, but I knew the problem. She was hungry, and I had nothing to feed her, not my own milk or any formula. The best I could do was try to muffle her cries in my chador.

Our door slammed shut, the lock closed, and the guard retreated up the stairs.

Click.

There was darkness.

Nothing but darkness.

A darkness so deep and complete that I wondered for a moment if I hadn't lost all power of sight.

I could see nothing at all. Not the bars at the end of my bed, not the hands, head, or anything else of Roksana that I held in front of my face.

Nothing.

I lay there, fearing that every creak and movement I heard was a rat coming to bite Roksana or Asghar come to hit me. I wanted to curl up tight and hide beneath a blanket, but I could already feel the lice and the fleas start to bite. I wanted to shout and beg to leave, but when the light was extinguished, so was my voice. The darkness was its own kind of torture—worse than anything Beautiful Hands could dream up.

———

When I finally calmed myself and gained a little courage, I removed my chador and tied it across the bars of the cell in the hope of maintaining some privacy whenever the lights were turned on again. In time, they were, and in came a guard I had never seen before. He was older than any of the others, with smeared glasses and rough skin. He pushed the chador aside and stood, staring at me for the longest time. His eyes made me long for the dark again.

Eventually, he walked back out and opened all the cells, letting the men stretch their legs. I followed them up the stairs to the first floor and into a dining room I had never seen before. The windows were painted over like they had been up on the fourth floor, but I could tell it was light outside, barely.

I joined a line to collect my food. There were hundreds of people, and from what I could see, every single one of them was a man. What little talking there was among them stopped as I shuffled forward. I didn't need to look up to know that many were looking at me.

The hush did not last long. As I followed Asghar to get my food the whole room erupted with angry shouts. I was not welcome. As a woman, my presence was an offense.

I looked up when I felt someone standing over me. He had a full beard and a loud voice. Staring at Asghar, he began to wave his arms at me. "She cannot eat with us," he said. "It is not acceptable for a woman to be here like this."

There were murmurs of agreement. Asghar glanced at me. "Let's go," he said, quietly.

Back in the cell with Asghar, I examined the food we had managed to gather: ten beans, just like there had been every other meal, a corner of flat bread, and a ladle of yogurt. Nothing for Roksana.

———

From that moment on, Roksana and I were confined to our cell. Asghar was allowed to go upstairs to collect our food and bring it back to the cell to eat with me. The only time I left the basement was when the guard allowed me to visit the bathroom. For the rest of the time, Roksana and I lay on our bunk, pinned down by the darkness.

The guards only turned the lights on when the men were taken to the dining hall or while someone was escorted to the bathroom. Gradually I grew accustomed to living in total darkness for twenty-two hours a day.

But I never fully lost the fear. Especially once the older guard started inviting Asghar up to the cell above ours to get drunk.

It happened for the first time a few days after we arrived in the basement. The men had just returned from eating, and I was picking my way through the ten beans, bread, and yogurt when the guard unlocked our cell, swung the door open, and stood, arms crossed, looking at Asghar.

"You look like you could enjoy a drink, friend," he said. "I have some *raki* upstairs if you'd like some."

Asghar swung his feet down from the bunk, puffed his chest, and followed him out. He didn't see the look the guard gave me as he pulled the door shut behind him and locked me back in.

As soon as I heard Asghar laughing upstairs I knew something was wrong. The guard had left the lights on, and Roksana was asleep. I pulled hard on the legs of the third bunk and managed to swing it out into the room. After a lot more pushing, pulling, and scraping of metal on concrete, I was able to haul it across the door, barricading the entrance. I tried to ignore the lifeless stares of the other inmates. As the sound of heavy footsteps thudded down from upstairs, I tied my chador up as a screen over my bunk, pulled Roksana close, and tried to hide. I pushed myself up against the wall, trying to stay out of sight. My heart was raging, and I could feel myself trembling against Roksana. I wished for the darkness to return so that I might become invisible again.

The key turned in the lock. I heard the sound of the bars pushing against the metal bed frame. Heard the guard breathing heavily from the effort as he pushed again and again. I buried my face in Roksana and begged silently for him to go away.

Finally, he paused. "Move the bed."

I stayed silent, my breath bottled up within me.

"Move the bed, now." He shoved again. I opened my eyes and peered through the gap in the chador. The bunk was moving a little but holding fast for now.

He exhaled. "Next time," he said. I listened to him leave, counting every one of his steps until I knew he was gone.

Click.

This time, the darkness brought relief.

———

When the lights were on I'd stare at the walls in the cell. They were covered in the names of different prisoners, as well as clusters of little vertical scratches, all arranged in rows of nine with a tenth line through the rest. I counted them carefully, looking for a clue as to how long we might be kept in there. Some added up to only a few weeks. Others were years.

I found a patch of wall and used a bit of broken wire from the bed to start my own tally of how many days we had been in the basement. Every day I added to it, I wondered how much more wall I would need.

After two days in the cell my milk came in again and I was finally able to feed Roksana myself. To my amazement, in all that time we were in the basement, she never got ill. Though there were fleas and filth all around us, not once did either of us get sick. She'd just lie on me, sleeping, feeding, or making gentle sounds of contentment and happiness. Sometimes I'd marvel that she would put up with such conditions. Then again, she'd spent the first nine months of her life within me, curled up in the darkness. Maybe curling up on top of me in the darkness now was the next best thing.

There was no bathroom down in the basement, but there

was a single tap. If I banged my bars loud enough to catch the attention of a guard I could wash my hands in the slow trickle of cold water. I used that tap to wash my hands, Roksana's tiny clothes, and even my pants as I wore them.

After so much washing, the fabric diaper I had been using eventually got so full of holes that it was no use at all. The only solution was to hold Roksana over an old milk bottle whenever the lights were on. She got so good at it that within a few weeks she would pee on demand.

Gradually I began to see that the other prisoners were not to be feared. Whenever I went to the tap to wash out some clothes I always made a point of offering to fill up the water bottles of some of the men in the other cells. They'd call me "sister" and thank me for my kindness. And when Asghar would disappear upstairs to get drunk, and I would start dragging the bunk across the floor, they'd shout their encouragement and jeer at the guard as he'd fail to push open the door.

It wasn't just the prisoners who protected me. Even one of the guards came down the stairs one night just after yet another attempt to break into my cell. "That man's thinking about you," he said. "He wants you. He's got a plan for you. Never go to the toilet alone, and never with him."

Even knowing they were looking out for me, though, it took even longer than usual that night for the shaking to stop and the fear to subside.

———

I had been in the basement for almost eight weeks when a female guard—the same one that had strip-searched me when I first arrived on the fourth floor—stood outside my cell and told me to hand Roksana over to Asghar and step outside.

"Why?" I asked.

"We're taking you for a bath."

I had been asking to wash properly with hot water for some days, but the thought of leaving Roksana with Asghar did not sit right with me. Still, I was in no position to argue. Though the interrogations by Beautiful Hands had stopped, barely a day went by without someone from the basement being hauled out and returned, an hour or two later, his face a swollen mess of blood. The air itself was heavy with the smell of infection as open wounds were left to fester and old injuries added to by the guards.

"Get out now!" the guard barked at me. I had no choice but to obey, to walk ahead of her as she pushed me out of the basement and into the cold air outside. The light was so bright that it hurt, and I flinched and stumbled like some kind of wounded animal. Unable to see where I was going, the guard grabbed me by the shoulders and pushed me into a car.

By the time I could open my eyes without the pain searing all the way back to my brain, the drive was over and I was standing inside a Turkish bathhouse. Just like in the dining room, the chatter of all the women stopped the moment I walked in. "She's from the prison," said my guard. Within minutes we were the only two left in the room.

The warm water felt good, even better than I had imagined it would when I lay in the darkness and felt the lice and fleas feast upon my blood. But even the luxury of being able to clean myself was not enough to quiet the questions that were causing me to panic inside. What was happening to Roksana while I was away? Why were they bathing me? Could I be sure that I was going to be taken back as soon as I was done? I stared at my bare body and noticed how thin I'd become. My body looked as though it belonged to a stranger who had lived far longer than I.

Again, the daylight was like acid in my eyes when I walked back to the car. And as I walked back down the stone steps and saw Roksana happily awake on Asghar's lap, I exhaled most of the tension I'd held within me.

Most, but not all. When the guard left me, I prepared myself for the inevitable slaps that Asghar would deliver.

From the moment we had been moved to the basement, Asghar's violence had been a regular part of life in the cell. If I joined in the singing that sometimes drifted across the basement in the darkness, he would tell me to shut up and slap me. If the men called me "sister" and thanked me for filling their water bottles, he would accuse me of being a whore and beat me. When I tried to warn him about the guard who tried to get him drunk, his anger flared up in an instant.

"That guard knows who I am," he said. "He understands that I am a very important man in Iran. That's why he respects me. That's why you're still safe."

Now that I was back in our cell, I braced myself. Inevitably, I felt his hand groping about in the darkness for my hair. As soon as he found it, he pulled so hard that I could feel great clumps tearing from my scalp. His other hand caught my cheek with a fierce slap. Two more followed in quick succession.

"I'm kind to you, Annahita, but you don't deserve it."

THE CLUSTER OF LINES ON THE WALL beside my bunk was growing. Each line represented another day spent in darkness, another day spent wondering how much longer we could be held like this. Another day listening for the warning signs that told me danger was about to strike.

But not every day was the same. Some lines had a story all their own. Like day sixty-two, when I made the trip to the bathhouse, or day eighty-one when a new prisoner was brought into the basement. He was a plumber and had helped one of the guards by fixing their heating at home. As a reward, the guard agreed to leave the lights on in the basement.

For three glorious days and nights, I could see everything. It didn't matter that I could now spot the roaches on the floor—just being able to see for so long was a blessing, and I was determined to make the most of it.

Since Roksana was no longer able to fit into the clothes that we had brought with us from Iran, I decided to ask a guard for a needle, thread, and scissors. He agreed to the needle, but that was all.

"But I need the scissors and thread too."

"Why?"

I held Roksana up. Her legs were poking through the holes I

had torn in the bottom of her onesie. "I can make her a dress, but I need some scissors."

The guard shrugged. "Maybe I can give you a razor."

When he came back later that day with the razor, I'd already picked enough thread from the thick blanket that we used to cover Roksana. Using a zipper from an old dress, some felt from another, a large square of material from the pair of pants that were too ripped for me to wear, I settled down and worked nonstop for the next twelve hours. I was hunched over on the bunk, Roksana lying in my lap, staring up in fascination at the colors and textures of the material that danced above her.

When the guard came back the next day, he was amazed to see Roksana wearing a beautiful pink dress that fit her perfectly.

———

Soon after I placed my one-hundredth scratch in the crumbling plaster next to my bunk, Asghar, Roksana, and I were joined by a new prisoner. Asghar slept through it all, but I watched, warily, as the guard pushed him in and he climbed up onto the one bunk that was not in use. It had been weeks since I'd had to drag it across the cell to prevent Asghar's drinking partner from getting in, but I felt the old fear return as our cell was once more handed over to the darkness.

"Why are you here with a baby?" he said softly. I could tell from his accent that he was from Tehran.

I thought about staying silent, guessing that Asghar would not like me talking to a strange man. But after so long in the basement, I was starting to wonder how much worse things could get. So I told him everything. Almost everything. I told him about the Smuggler and the mountains and how we had been picked up by the guards on the border and how they had been so kind at first, but how things had soon changed.

There was silence after I finished speaking. "I've heard many stories of people dying in the mountains," he said quietly. "And I've heard stories about other families in here over the years. One of them came in with two children but left with only one. Another time there was a woman in here, but she ended up getting killed."

I could hear the tremor in my voice as I spoke. "How do you know about that?"

"They've got me in here because they think I'm a smuggler, but I'm not. I just import things from Germany and take them back home. But I've met enough people as I've driven to hear all about this place. You need to get out of here. You're not safe."

"I know. But how?"

"I can help."

The next day, as the men returned from breakfast, Asghar and our new cellmate were talking under their breath about how dangerous the Hotel was for us. I was relieved that Asghar was listening to him, that it was clear that he respected and trusted him. The conversation died as soon as the guard came down to lock us in, but the whispers began again as the lights went out.

"I've paid my way out of here by giving one of the guards my trailer. I swear on my father's grave that I will help you get out when I'm gone."

I wanted to believe him, but instead of his promise filling me with hope, his description of the danger I was in filled me with fear. From that moment on, I no longer worried that the scratches in the wall might go on indefinitely. I was terrified that the guards might kill me.

When the guards came for him the next day, the man handed me a bag of pistachios. "I'll do what I said," he whispered. "I promise."

FIFTEEN DAYS AFTER OUR CELLMATE left, the light clicked on, the lock sprung open, and a guard stood and delivered the words I had feared I would never hear: "It's time to go."

Minutes later, I was standing with Asghar and Roksana in the courtyard. Roksana was crying at the brightness of the late afternoon sunlight. In between comforting her and allowing my own eyes to readjust, I tried to look around and find out what was going on. "Where are we going?" I asked the guard, but he ignored me.

We were put in a car, along with two Afghan men, and were driven a short distance to a bus station. A few minutes later the five of us were sitting on the bus with two guards behind us, pulling out of town and heading for Istanbul.

Neither of the guards wanted to talk to us that much, but after a few miles Asghar did manage to get one of them to talk.

"When we get to Istanbul we'll take you to register at a police station."

"What then? Are we free?"

The guard smirked and shrugged. "You should get some sleep. It's a long drive."

It took almost a whole day and night in all. I slept when I could, but the combination of hunger and anxiety about what was coming next kept me awake most of the time. I tried to distract myself by looking out at the mountain ravines we edged around and the valley roads we snaked along, but my mind would never let me go too long without imagining what Istanbul might hold. Would the police station be just another gateway to prison, just as it had been when we first arrived in the country? Or would we really be free after all? Without any money, any papers, or anyone in the city we knew, who we could call on for help? How free would we really be?

It was getting dark again by the time we approached Istanbul. The sky above glowed orange from miles away, and as we drove down wide freeways and over tall bridges, I could see the city, so full of life, beckoning us.

It was a short, cold walk from the bus stop to the police station. The guards who had traveled with us told us to sit on a bench by the wall, talked briefly with an officer behind the desk, sparked up a cigarette each, and then left.

The two Afghan men were called up first. Asghar and I watched, trying to work out what was going on, but even though it was late the station was too busy and noisy for us to hear what they were being told. After signing some papers, one of them was handed a telephone and allowed to make a call before being sent back to sit near us.

"You, come here," said the man behind the desk, jabbing a fat finger in our direction.

He had a file in front of him with two pages in it. Even though I had learned enough Turkish over the last few months to understand what he was saying, I had not yet learned how to decipher the strange script in which it was written.

He asked our names, dates of birth, and a few more basic details.

"Sign here," he said, looking about him, as bored as any official I had ever encountered in my life.

"Okay," he said, taking the sheets back after we had followed his instruction. "You can go."

I looked at Asghar, hoping he understood what was going on, but he looked as confused as me.

"We're free?" I asked.

The man had already cleaned up our papers and was opening up another file. "Yes," he hissed, without taking his eyes off the papers in front of him. "Of course you're free. Go."

We went back to the bench. It was strange, but I didn't feel elated or even all that relieved. I just felt tired. Exhausted, as if my body had reached the end of the longest walk it had ever done. All I wanted to do was stop for a while. I lay down and let all the lights and the noise and the warmth of the air wash me off to sleep.

"Get up!" The guard was shouting at us from behind the desk. "Go out!"

"Where to?" said Asghar.

"I don't care where you go. You can't stay here."

I stumbled to my feet, feeling confused and unsure for a moment even which country I was in. Before we made it to the door, one of the Afghan men we had left the Hotel with called out.

"Do you need somewhere to stay tonight?"

Within minutes of walking into the house, I felt as though I could stay awake forever. There were parents and sisters and cousins and grandparents, all gathered to greet the two men from Afghanistan who had finally arrived home. There was food, music, and dancing, and the air was soon thick with cries of joy and celebration. The family welcomed the three of us as if we were their own, and as I watched it struck me that this was exactly the kind of party that Mohammad and I had wanted to throw to celebrate our first year of marriage.

Sleep came upon me that night like a winter fog, but when I awoke the next day I did not feel free or as if my days in the prison were behind me. There was still a blanket of foreboding over me, a lack of peace I could not quite identify. All I knew was that another stage of the journey was about to begin.

Even though the police had made it clear that we could go and that they didn't have much interest in where we ended up, the choices ahead of us were limited. We could have asked to stay with the family awhile longer, but what would happen when their hospitality ran out? Could we really expect to find work and a place to live in a matter of days? Besides, four months in a Turkish jail had shown us just how the authorities viewed illegal immigrants like us. Neither of us wanted to stay in Turkey any longer than we had to. Our best option was to declare ourselves refugees and hope that some country would help.

We got a ride from our hosts to the refugee center and spent the whole day waiting between interviews with different officials. By the time we were shown upstairs to a room with two beds, I was too tired and hungry to notice much more than the fact that there were clean floors and a light switch that we could control ourselves.

People stared when I sat in the dining room and started putting food into my mouth. I barely registered the taste of the meal or the looks of sympathy on people's faces. When I had been weighed earlier in the day the nurse had looked concerned. I was barely ninety pounds.

———

A kind Roma woman visited our room early the next morning, bringing with her a saucepan of warm stew. It was hard to understand each other, but between us we knew enough Turkish for her to tell me that she was worried about how thin I looked and wanted to help if she could. She fussed over Roksana while Asghar took the saucepan and went in search of a spoon.

I thought about what she could help me with. Almost 150 days had passed since I had tried to force a smile as I said goodbye to Daniel in Isfahan. So far, I had been grateful that he had been spared the horrors of the mountain or the trials of the prison. But now, as I realized that those dangers were past, a deep, primal hunger awoke within me. I had to see my son again. I had to do everything I possibly could so that we might be reunited.

"Can I borrow some money?" I asked. "I need to phone my son."

She smiled and handed me some liras. It was the first Turkish money that I had seen. I thanked her and quickly put it in my pocket before Asghar returned.

———

"Dad?"

"Annahita?" The relief in his voice was clear. He paused a moment. When he spoke again, the warmth was gone. "Where are you?"

"We're in Istanbul." I wanted to tell him everything, to let him know the truth about why two seasons had passed since I had left Daniel with him. But I knew I had to keep up the lie, for my parents' and Daniel's sake.

"Roksana is growing big," I said, hoping to fill the silence. "How is Daniel? Can I speak with him?"

"You ask about Daniel? You left him, Annahita. You went off with your husband, and you left your son behind. You decided that your husband was worth more to you than your son, so you chose to forget about Daniel. How can you call yourself Daniel's mom now? You don't deserve him. Your son doesn't even like you anymore, and I doubt he'll want to speak to you at all."

I cried and cried. I was using a public phone in a shop, but there was nothing I could do to hold the pain in. Every word that my dad said was like poison. Soon I was struggling even for breath.

"Annahita?" my dad said, his anger softening a little. I could hear him calling my name over and over, but still I could not stop weeping. Finally, when I was able to wrestle back the tears just a little, he spoke again. "Do you want to speak to Daniel?"

"Yes," I whispered.

I heard the phone clunk down on the table and my dad's voice call out to my son. "Daniel, come."

I pictured Daniel playing with his toys by the door that opened onto the courtyard. I saw him stand up and walk over to the phone, picking it up shyly. Maybe my mom's hand was on his shoulder, telling him it was okay to talk.

But all I heard was silence.

"Daniel," my dad called again. "Come here."

Someone covered the receiver then, and the conversation that carried on was hidden from me.

"Annahita," my dad said finally. "Daniel doesn't want to talk to you. I'm sorry."

I could feel the same darkness from the basement invade my head and heart again. Whatever happiness I'd felt at getting away from the Hotel and being able to phone home was extinguished that instant.

All I felt was despair.

———

The heartbreak did not fade, but life continued. I had traded the life of a prisoner for the life of a refugee, and in this new world we were free to come and go in the refugee center. But, with no money at first, we still spent much of our time in the room. There were days when I wondered how much really had changed since we left the Hotel.

In time, though, our situation improved. I was able to earn a little money by sewing clothes for some of the other refugees in the center. I had no machine or desk to work at, but Roksana's little pink dress had taught me that I didn't need either of those in order to work.

Asghar, too, had something to distract him, and he would spend hours away from the room, without ever telling me where he went. I didn't mind at all, for by now I was content to sit and sew and watch Roksana as she crawled about on the floor, building towers out of plastic beakers and laughing with delight whenever they crashed down.

I phoned my parents every week, and, even though Daniel refused to speak to me, after two weeks in Istanbul I had finally been able to hear his voice. Khanoum had sent me a recording of him on cassette, and I had been given an old tape player by one of the center workers. Every day I listened to him talk about the toys he was playing with and the animals he thought were the best in the whole world. His voice was like fresh blood in my veins, giving me strength to work as hard as I could to be reunited with him. But it also cut deep within me, for in one part of the tape I could hear Daniel crying, then screaming out, "I want my mommy!"

I was desperate to see him again, and I eventually worked out a plan to make it happen.

Asghar and I had applied to Denmark for asylum, as we had been advised they were taking refugees, but we knew it would take months for our appointment to come through. So, in the meantime, I worked on my side plan, which involved a man who I hoped could help.

He was called Agha Danesh and was a businessman from Isfahan who regularly traveled back to Istanbul. My dad had known him for years and asked him to bring some supplies back to us. Soon after that first phone call, we met outside the refugee center one afternoon.

"Your parents are worried about you," Agha Danesh said as he handed over a leather bag full of clothes and food and other supplies. "They can't sleep."

"Did you see my son Daniel when you collected the bag?"

"Yes. He's a good boy." He paused a little, searching for the right words. "But he is sad." Agha Danesh turned to leave, but then he stopped. "You know, I can help you get him out. The border guards know me well enough not to ask questions if I don't want them to."

Back in our room, Asghar pulled out a pair of scissors and cut away at the lining of the bag. "Ha!" he said, pulling out a load of bills my father had told us he was going to sew in. "This is good!"

I just watched him in silence. I didn't care that he was taking the cash and that I'd probably never see it again. I didn't want money. I didn't want my father to send items that would simply help us get by in Istanbul. I just wanted Daniel. That was all.

I wanted my son so badly that I was prepared to do anything to get him out.

———

The next time I phoned home, I laid out the plan for my dad. I told him about how Agha Danesh could bribe the border guards and bring Daniel back to Istanbul.

"No," he said. "That is not a good idea. I hear that the border is a dangerous place and that many people end up going missing. I trust Agha Danesh but not the guards. It's better that you get to Denmark first; then I can get Daniel a passport and visa and bring him out properly."

It was hard to disagree, but I knew what this meant. Getting a passport in Iran would take a whole year, and then another six months for a visa. At this rate, I would end up missing two years of my son's life.

I tried to stay calm, to reason with my dad, but it was no use. He said that his and my mom's minds were made up and there was no way they were going to smuggle Daniel out of the country. "Besides," he added, "even if he does arrive there safely, are you sure that your husband will take care of him?"

I kept my emotions inside while we talked, but once the conversation was over I exploded. Again, right there in the shop,

I was once more a mess of tears. My parents had a right to be worried, both about smuggling and what life with Asghar would be like. But my heart ached for Daniel. Even though I knew that Asghar was dangerous, Iran was worse. The longer Daniel stayed there, the more likely he'd be exposed to the growing threats under Khomeini's regime. I wanted Daniel with me in Turkey, where I could hold him, care for him, and protect him.

The tears kept on coming. But I wasn't just crying for Daniel. I was crying for Mohammad, too, for everything that Roksana had been through, and for all the fear and despair that had settled so heavily in my own heart.

A week or two later I was back at the shop, waiting in line at the counter to buy a comb for Roksana. When it was my turn to pay I stepped up and smiled at the shopkeeper.

"You must pay what you owe me first before you can buy anything else," he said.

"I don't think I owe you any money. You know I always pay when I come in and use the phone or buy things."

"Your husband doesn't, though. Look," he said, pulling out a bill from beneath the counter. It was a long list of cigarettes and Johnny Walker whiskey, things I'd never bought in my life but that I knew Asghar had developed a taste for. The final amount was as much as I had earned from a month of sewing clothes, money that I had been saving to pay Agha Danesh to get Daniel out, if my parents ever changed their minds. I handed it over and left.

I was enraged all the way back to the center, and when I walked into our room and saw Asghar lying on the bed, I shouted at him. "How dare you go and buy all that stuff in the shop and expect me to pay! I was saving that for Daniel, but as fast as I'm earning it you're smoking and drinking it away."

"Who are you to tell me right from wrong?" he spat back at me. "And who are you to talk about Daniel? You never say anything about Cherie, never say anything about wanting to get her back. You're not a mother. You're nothing."

It had been weeks since he had hit me, but as soon as his fists shot out toward my shoulder and chest, I remembered exactly what it had felt like before. I was back in the cell in the basement, cowering in the darkness. I was back in the kitchen in Isfahan, hiding among the broken glass as he brought the shovel down on me again and again.

He stopped when there was a knock on the door and a voice I didn't know asked to come in. Asghar opened the door and walked right out.

It was 3 a.m. when he came back again. I could smell the booze and cigarettes before he had even stepped into the room. I braced myself for more pain, but he was too drunk and tired for that.

"You've got another bill to pay off," he said, before lying down on the bunk next to me. Within minutes he was snoring. Only then did I let myself cry. Once I started, I couldn't stop.

Seven months after arriving in Istanbul, we finally received news that we had been accepted by Denmark. They sent us visas, one-way plane tickets, and the promise of a new life in a country where I would finally be free from the oppression of an Islamic regime. No more chadors, no more prisons, no more fear of the mullahs. But I wasn't quite ready yet to embrace this freedom.

"I'm not going," I told my friends in the center. "I'm not leaving here until Daniel is with me."

Over the coming weeks so many people tried to change my mind. They told me how good life would be in Denmark, how I could send for Daniel once I was there, how life for him would be so much better in Europe. "No," I repeated time after time. "I am not going without my child."

My refusal to leave was not a show of strength or an attempt to bargain with my dad or the authorities. I was fifteen hundred miles away from my son already. I simply could not put any more distance between us. If I left Turkey and headed farther west, I feared my heart would break completely.

I knew that our tickets were only valid for two months, and I knew that, yet again, I had no choice in the matter. And so, just days before the window of a new life closed, I changed my mind. Not that I feared the pain any less or that I found a way to see some great hope in the situation. I simply hoped that somehow my soul would be able to cope with the pain.

———

The last-night party that my friends threw for us in our room at the center was nice. There was singing and a little dancing, and Roksana was passed around the women and smothered with kisses until she giggled herself red. I felt like I could breathe a little more easily that night, as if the air was cleaner and purer somehow.

That night reminded me of what I really wanted—to make

a safe home and a good future for my son and my daughter. I wanted all of us to be able to live without having to hold our breaths in fear of what was coming next.

I wanted to belong too. To be able to laugh and dance and hear the air fill with the laughter and happy talk of people I knew and loved.

But I knew all this would have to wait.

On the morning that we left, I looked at the single green suitcase we had been given. The empty shelves and walls all around told me that we had left nothing behind. But my heart felt the ache of what was missing. What little we had we carried between us.

As we left the center, I did not feel like I was starting a new adventure. The burning sickness in my stomach and the stone in my throat told a different story. The room was empty and my bag was full, but I felt as though I was leaving everything behind.

PART THREE

DENMARK AND SWEDEN

I HUNG UP THE PHONE AND WEPT FOR
the twelfth time. Roksana sat on my foot and hugged my shin,
begging me to stand up and take her for a ride around the room.
I did as she asked, dragging my foot along the floor as she
squealed with delight. I laughed a little through the tears, but
the pain within remained just as sharp.

It was spring, and we had been in Denmark for six months
already. We had been given two rooms in a large house up in
the northeastern corner of the country. We shared the bathroom and kitchen with two other refugee families, and life had
quickly developed a sense of routine. Asghar and I both spent
much of our time out of the house, Asghar in the company of
other Iranian men in the area, talking up a storm but not doing
much else. He had already given up on the Danish lessons that
the state had encouraged us to take. I, on the other hand, had
enrolled at a local college where I spent a few hours most days,
sitting in bright, clean classrooms, working hard to master this
strange new language.

Some evenings Asghar would barge into the living room and
inform me that he had invited twenty of his friends over later
that night and that he had promised them a good meal. I quickly
learned not to argue or make a fuss. Instead I'd scrape together

what little money I had hidden and head quickly to the shop to buy rice, tomatoes, and whatever cuts of meat I could afford.

Besides the school work, the household chores, and the regular outbursts of rage from Asghar, there was one other routine that dominated everything: my phone calls home.

My parents no longer owned a phone, so they had to reserve a thirty-minute period at the local phone house to talk with me. Every other week, as the set hour approached, I would picture them making the short drive in Dad's old car. I always imagined that Daniel would be happily watching out the window as the streets rolled by, his eyes curious about the world he lived in.

I always spoke to Dad first. I would ask about the passport applications that would allow him, Mom, and Daniel to finally come to Denmark, hoping for news that never came. He had softened a little since we had left Turkey, but his voice still carried a note of disapproval. In his mind, I had chosen a no-good, violent husband over my own son. It hurt him to think that his own daughter could be so selfish and blind.

Mom was always warmer. She would ask about Roksana and me, wanting to know what life was like in Denmark. She always cooed whenever I told her about the size of the supermarkets or the bright clothes that the women wore in public.

Eventually, when my heart was beating so fast within me that my voice began to shake, I would say the words I had rehearsed so many times. "Let me speak to Daniel."

For the first five and a half months that we had been in Denmark, the line would go dead as muffled voices would fog the background. Eventually Dad would return and I would spend the remaining minutes of the call forcing back tears.

This time, our twelfth call, things were different.

My brother, Hussein, had gone with them to the phone house. I didn't have to ask him to get Daniel; he knew right away. He didn't cover the receiver either, and I heard him clearly.

"Daniel, you need to talk to your mother. Come here."

I heard the phone creak and the shift as it was passed from one hand to another.

I heard him breathing.

"Daniel?"

Silence.

"Daniel? It's me, your mom. Are you there?"

I listened hard. No words, but the breathing remained. It was him. I knew it was him.

But the silence grew steadily heavier.

"Daniel, I love you. I miss you, Daniel."

Silence.

"You're coming to Denmark, and everything's going to be okay."

For two minutes he said nothing. I cried and told him over and over how much I loved him and how much I was looking forward to seeing him again, but I heard nothing but his breathing coming down the line.

When I did finally hear a voice, it was Mom's. She said that she loved me and that the time was up.

I heard the line go dead. Sorrow flowed out of me like a flood. I gathered Roksana to my chest and fought for air in between heaving sobs.

I viewed life in Denmark through the lens of my sorrow. I noticed the vast differences between life there and life back in Iran but nothing moved me. The best new foods and the most exciting new tastes were bland upon my tongue. There was no joy in the world, no excitement, nothing to thrill me.

I noticed that people in Denmark were so different from people in Iran or Turkey. There was no visible anger in them, no hate raging just beneath the surface. When people disagreed in public, there were no shouts or screams or threats backed up with guns and knives. Things were gentle, warm, and easy.

I compared myself to the Danes all the time, wondering how different my life would have been had I been born in the flat suburbs of Copenhagen instead of the mountains around Isfahan. But even though this new life had so much more to offer, I missed some of the parts of my life back in Iran. When I heard Iranians talk, I'd often cry. When I thought of certain songs or smelled saffron rice, I was reminded how far away from home I was. I knew I didn't belong anywhere.

Most of all, though, my life was dominated by the ache of missing Daniel.

I would entertain daydreams of smuggling Daniel out of Iran, of getting him to Turkey and somehow bringing him back to be with me and Roksana in Denmark. But I knew these were foolish ideas. Dad would never agree to it. And did I really want to risk Daniel at the border crossing?

All I could do was wait and hope that in the year it would take for Mom, Dad, and Daniel to get their passports, nothing would go wrong.

As the months passed, the sorrow shifted a little. Not that it got any easier. Instead of feeling depressed, I started to feel angry at myself. Angry for leaving Daniel. Angry for marrying Asghar. Angry for finding myself in a position where I had no choice but to smile and pretend like everything was all perfectly normal as I waved to my son from the back of the car window.

How could I have let all this happen?

⸺

Once I had learned enough Danish, I was able to study other subjects at college. I added math, English, and geography to my class schedule and found the work to be a welcome distraction. Sometimes, like when I felt my wrist ache from writing page after page of notes, or when I sat on the floor at home surrounded by piles of books, nursing a cup of black, sweet tea, or when I was laughing at a joke made by one of my classmates in the canteen at break, I felt something I'd not experienced for years. I felt like a normal person my age.

I was twenty-one years old. In Iran it was perfectly normal to have two or more children by that age. But in Denmark the rules were different. Even though a lot of the people I studied with were older, I saw enough twenty-year-olds around the college to know that they were carefree and funny, like slightly taller versions of their adolescent selves, only with money to spend and cars to drive. I knew I could never be like them, but for just a few moments every week, I could at least pretend.

Because I dropped Roksana off at day care while I studied, nobody knew I was a mother. I told no one about my life, so nobody knew that I was married either. Not that anyone ever asked. It suited me fine, for though I had my moments when I liked to pretend that I was one of them, I could always hear Asghar's voice loud in my head.

"Don't look to the Danish people, and don't ever make friends with them," he'd say whenever we were out together, usually for me to act as his translator if he had to visit the doctor or run some other errand that placed too many demands on his limited Danish vocabulary. "We're Persian, so don't make friends with them. Look to me instead."

The more time he spent with his Iranian friends, the more involved he got in politics. He would deliver long lectures about the failings of Khomeini's regime and talk endlessly about the way he and his friends were going to help get the Shah back into power. In their minds, at least, they were still fighting. But from what I heard when I cleaned up after them as they sat around our home, it seemed they were spending less time fighting the regime and more time jostling among each other for power.

Asghar's loyalist group kept him busy, but it did not keep him calm. He still raged and ranted, still lashed out whenever he was displeased. If I got upset about Daniel, he would shout at me. If Roksana played too loudly, he would shout at her. And if the shouting did not satisfy him, which it rarely ever did, he would use his fists.

—

Ever since we had married Asghar had called me a whore. He accused me of being unfaithful with so many different people, I grew a little deaf to it. But as I put more effort into my studies, I guess it was only inevitable that he would start to focus on the people I was with at college.

"Where were you at noon today?" he asked one evening.

It was an unusual question, and it caught me off guard. "I had English," I said, my voice a little weak.

"Which room were you in?"

I told him the number and went back to feeding Roksana.

The next night, as soon as he came home, he was wild. "Why do you lie to me?" he shouted, slamming a dish out of my hand and sending it crashing into the wall. "What are you trying to hide?"

"Nothing," I said, my eyes looking down far enough to appear submissive, but remaining high enough to be able to spot the next attack.

"I came to the room today at twelve, and you were not there. Who were you with? You are your teacher's whore, yes?"

I tried to explain the way that college worked, how we moved from classroom to classroom for each lesson, but it did no good. Nothing I could say would stop him.

The next day one of my tutors called me to one side. "Annahita, is your dad going to visit today?"

I looked at her, confused. "My dad?"

"Yes, he was here yesterday. The office says that he comes a lot. It's really disruptive, you know."

"I know, but he's not my dad. He's my husband." I watched her face freeze for a moment, then snap back into life. When she spoke again, she put her hand on my shoulder. I winced a little as the bruised flesh cried out. "Okay, well, you have to stop him, Annahita. We can't have him coming here and peering into all the classrooms like he does."

I wondered for a moment what would happen if I told her everything. Would she believe me? Could she help? Would it even make any difference at all? As far as I could tell, the only outcome would be a lot more violence. So I bit my tongue.

———

By the time the academic year ended, we had been in Denmark for nine months. We had moved out of the shared house and into an apartment of our own on the outskirts of Copenhagen. It was a little bigger than the two rooms we had before, and I liked the fact that there was a playground outside that I could easily see from the kitchen window up there on the third floor. As summer brought with it long evenings and warm days, I liked to daydream about watching Daniel and Roksana playing on the swings together.

I had enrolled at a new college and found it to be just as warm and friendly as the previous one. As the semester drew to a close, somehow I had let slip to Asghar that I had been invited to an end-of-year party run by the faculty. I told him I wasn't going, but he surprised me when he asked why not.

"You won't like it," I said. I must have been especially tired because my tongue then got a little loose. "You'll just accuse me of being with other men. It's not worth the pain."

Asghar drew himself up to his full height, donned a serious expression, and nodded a little. He looked like he was audition-ing for the role of high court judge in a badly acted television show. "No, no, no," he said, his hands held out wide. "You must go. I will borrow from one of my friends, and I will drive you."

I didn't like this game. It was new and unpredictable. "No, Asghar. I'm not going."

"Yes, you are. You must go."

I had no choice. Even when he didn't manage to borrow his friend's car for the night he still insisted that I go. He had never behaved like that before, and it left me confused. Perhaps that was why I accepted the glass of red wine that was pressed into my hand. It was the first time I had ever tasted it, and soon my head was a little light and my balance a little off.

He could still smell it on me as soon as I walked back into our apartment. He stood up and walked toward me, eyes locked, sniffing as though he were a wolf and I a wounded lamb.

"You drank alcohol?"

I started to explain, but his hand stung my cheek before I could get the words out. He grabbed my hair and dragged me toward the bedroom. My feet couldn't keep up. I could feel the skin coming away from the top of my head.

He pushed me onto the bed. I tried to hide, to make myself small and protect myself with the pillows and the covers, but he grabbed me again. He was shouting at the top of his voice, calling me every obscenity imaginable. Reaching under the bed he pulled out a stick as thick as my wrist and as long as my leg. He had always said that he had it to protect us from intruders, but that night he lifted it high to strike me.

———

I was supposed to return to the college the next day to talk about the next year and hand in some paper work. I had spent most of the night in the bathroom, watching the bruises emerge across my chest, arms, side, and legs. I had a cut across my face that had barely stopped bleeding and a black eye that was already swollen. No amount of makeup would cover it up, and whenever I tried to walk, my steps were those of an old woman.

When it was time to leave the apartment, I phoned my teacher instead. Asghar was asleep and I was desperate not to wake him, but as soon as the cheery female voice on the other end said my name, I started to cry.

"What's wrong?"

"I'm okay. I have just been sick in the night. Can I mail you the paperwork?"

"Of course," she said. A long pause followed. "We want to help you, Annahita."

I knew that she spoke the truth, and I didn't doubt that she cared, but what could she do? There was no way she could help. And deep inside, a part of me doubted that I even deserved to be rescued. The words I had heard after Mohammad's death—that God was punishing me—still continued to haunt me.

I couldn't understand what I had done to deserve Mohammad's death, but if I abandoned my husband, what would God do to me then? I was terrified of God, terrified of causing further shame for my family back home. That fear kept me trapped more than any bars of any cell I had been kept behind in Turkey.

The only thing I could do was hide. I hid my story from my fellow students and teachers, as well as from my parents. I hid my bruises behind makeup and my sorrow behind hard work. I hid my hope of seeing Daniel from Asghar, for fear of making him mad. I hid from Roksana my fear that one day he would turn on his own daughter.

I was hiding everything. Soon there would be nothing left.

I HAD ALREADY DECIDED NOT TO GO outside the morning that someone knocked at the door. I checked the spy hole. A man and woman stood there, both wearing smart suits and holding briefcases. I panicked. If they were from immigration it couldn't be good news. If they were here about last night's fight, it could be even worse. I stuck to my plan and backed quietly away from the door.

The wounds I had received at the start of the summer had long since faded, but the previous night had brought a fresh batch of sharp pain in my muscles and deep red marks across my skin. Most of the time Asghar stuck to body shots, but from time to time he favored a black eye or a cut cheek. Last night I had gotten both.

The move to Copenhagen had brought us into contact with new friends. They were still Iranian, naturally, and it was only ever Asghar who invited people over to visit with us. But as we sat around and I listened to Asghar talk with the couple who had recently arrived from our homeland, I was reminded of what a normal life for a married couple was like. They were relaxed and talked easily about the life they had left behind and the future they were hoping for. I remembered talking like that with Mohammad. It was a lifetime ago.

Whatever calm was in the room did not last. As the

conversation turned to politics and Asghar's role in the fight to put the Shah back in power, the atmosphere grew tense. I wasn't even following the discussion anymore. I had seen the twist of Asghar's jaw and the set of his eyes. I knew what was coming.

Soon Asghar had shed his polite skin and was standing up, shouting at me for letting the tea go cold. The couple dropped their eyes to the ground, so they didn't see Asghar reach into his pocket and pull out the gray-handled box cutter. But I did. I knew it was only a matter of time before he held it up in front of his face, pushed up the blade, and said, "Your father never taught you anything. So now it's my turn."

Asghar had been carrying the knife for a couple of weeks. He hadn't cut me yet, but as he wrapped his fingers around it and punched me hard in the chest, I felt a new level of pain in my ribs.

Our guests had shouted at him to stop. The husband tried to take the knife, and the wife stood in the gap between Asghar and me. That gave me the time to run to the bathroom and hide. I listened to him curse them out until they reluctantly left. When Asghar broke the lock, there was nothing I could do.

———

The knock at the door was insistent. Asghar hadn't come home since he'd left in the middle of the night, and in an instant I decided to change my mind. After all, I said to myself as I opened the door, how much worse could things get?

I could barely understand anything they said. They spoke English, not Danish, and I could only pick out a few words. "God . . . Jesus . . . book . . ."

"I not speak English. Speak Farsi," I said, trying to remember the words for "Can you repeat that slower please?" They smiled a lot and carried on talking about God and Jesus, but soon it was obvious that the conversation was going nowhere.

"Tomorrow?" the woman said, looking hopeful. "Here?"

I said yes, though I didn't really know what to, and closed the door.

When they knocked the next day, it was raining hard, but their smiles were just as bright. They didn't try to talk too much, but instead the woman handed me a book. She clasped her hands together in front of her chest, and then they both said good-bye.

I shut the door and looked at the slab of paper and leather in my hands. I recognized the script as Farsi, my native tongue. It was a Bible. When I skimmed the pages, I struggled to understand the words, for even though I recognized the letters, the words themselves were so old and antiquated that the sentences barely made any sense at all.

Great, I thought. *What do I do with this?* I couldn't read the thing, so I could see no point in keeping it. But could I throw it away? Surely that would really anger God. For years I'd been trying to block out the fear that God might be punishing me. So I put the Bible at the top of the bookcase. It was one more thing to try and forget about.

Asghar spent more and more time with the supporters of the Shah. Sometimes I was grateful for the amount of time it took him away from home, but as much as it helped it also harmed. From the little he told me, there were constant struggles for power within the group. When he felt as though his influence was fading, his temper at home grew even worse.

A few months after I was given the Bible, Asghar returned home in just such a mood. He started an argument about my cooking, and it soon developed into a tirade against my character. It was the same words and the same hatred that I had heard a hundred times before, but this time, as he accused me of spreading rumors about him among the group and stormed back out of the house, I did something I had never done before. I reached up to the top of the bookcase and pulled down the Bible. For the first time ever, I prayed.

"If you are there, please show him that it wasn't me."

I don't know why I reached for the Bible, why I prayed, or why I kissed it before putting it back. I had barely thought about God since Mohammad's death; only when I was at my lowest point and begged him for a swift death. All the rest of the time I was too busy surviving to wonder whether God cared at all about my life.

But in the moment that I held the Bible to my face and smelled the old leather and fresh printed pages, something within me shifted. Somewhere deep inside I was admitting that I needed him. It was a tiny move on my part, a microscopic event. It wasn't even a step of faith so much as an act of desperation.

And when Asghar returned a few hours later and apologized for accusing me falsely, I was stunned.

IT TOOK A YEAR FOR MY PARENTS AND
Daniel to get their passports and half as long again for the
Danish embassy to issue visas. It had been two and a half years
total since I had said good-bye to my son. So when the day finally
came and my dad called with the news that they were ready to
travel, I needed several minutes to let the words sink in.

Soon I was crying with joy and relief, picking Roksana up
and whirling her around the apartment, telling her that at last
her big brother was going to come and live with us.

I had a month to prepare before their arrival, and I threw
myself into the tasks ahead of me. I made enquiries to enroll
Daniel in a school, painted his room, and found him a bed
that was being thrown out as scrap by one of our neighbors. I
searched the Goodwill stores for new clothes and asked anyone I
knew with a son what seven-year-old boys liked best.

Ever since marrying Asghar I had struggled to sleep properly,
but now instead of fear keeping me awake, it was nothing but
pure happiness that robbed me of sleep.

Even Asghar joined in. "I will be a good father to him," he
said, more than once. "And when Cherie comes, too, we will
finally be a family again." I was too happy to question his prom-
ises and too distracted to wonder how he really would react to

Daniel's return. All that mattered was that my boy was coming back.

—

It was almost painful to stand at the arrivals gate in the Copenhagen airport, scrutinizing the bodies shuffling through the doors. So many times I thought it was them, only to be disappointed. I could feel the air grow heavy within me, feel my breathing quicken and my hands get clammy as they curled around Roksana's. It had been too long, all but a month of Roksana's lifetime.

When I finally saw them—my parents pushing a trolley laden with cases—there was no sign of Daniel. I strained to get a better look, confused at what might have happened, my hands clasped tight against my chest. Then I saw his feet, fumbling along behind the trolley. My son's feet, walking toward me.

Dad pushed the trolley ahead as they cleared the barriers, and I finally got to see all of my boy. He had grown so tall and looked so handsome. A million fireworks exploded within me as I knelt down to greet him. Tears soaking my face, I threw my arms wide and called out his name. "Daniel! Daniel! My son!"

Mom guided him forward, and he stood, cold and still. I held him tight, but it was like embracing a ghost.

Even though Daniel had been avoiding my calls all this time, I had thought, somewhere in the back of my mind, that we just needed to be reunited physically and everything would fall into place. But things were not that simple. All the joy and hope that had been bubbling over soured that instant. All that was left was disappointment, pain, and confusion. How could I reach my boy? He was closed to me. Everything was locked away. Had the cord between us been broken forever? I loved him still, there was no doubt about it, but could he ever love me again? Could I ever gain back his trust?

I opened my eyes and looked up. I wanted to compose myself before saying a few words, but I stopped short when I saw Asghar staring at the two of us, his face enraged. I remembered again the jealousy which had burned within him whenever I had hugged Daniel in Isfahan. I remembered the way he hated it whenever I showed Daniel any kind of affection. The memory made me shiver.

—

Back in the apartment, we settled into a strange version of family life. I was desperate to break through to Daniel but also fearful of what might happen if Asghar allowed his anger to surface. I could tell that Mom and Dad were watching Asghar carefully, wondering whether it was safe to leave Daniel with him. Roksana reacted as any two-and-a-half-year-old would to the sudden arrival of an older brother and grandparents—sometimes with joy and sometimes with frustration. Daniel showed no sign of warming to me, and I noticed him freezing whenever Asghar was near him.

The stress was palpable, and I worked hard to make sure Asghar had no cause to complain about anything, from the food I served to the way I spoke to him. Because I had made my dad Daniel's legal guardian before we left Iran, he could still take him back home if he wished. Twin fears stalked me: the possibility of losing Daniel again if my parents refused to leave him with me and the possibility of seeing Daniel hurt if my parents *did* choose to leave him with me. What would happen when my parents' three months were up and they returned home? How much longer would Asghar's anger remain in check?

My dad and mom were asking the same question, almost outright at times. "Is Asghar treating you well?" they asked, more than once, but only when he was out of the apartment. "What happened to you in Turkey? Why did you not call for all those months?"

I was so used to hiding the truth from everyone around me, the lies came easily.

———

Though there were times when Roksana was excited to have a new big brother in her home, she did not always take kindly to Daniel's presence. On the first night he was with us, she put his bag, coat, and shoes outside the front door, exclaiming loudly in Danish, "She's *my* mommy."

Daniel started school within a week of his arrival. I was nervous, especially when his teacher informed me that in Daniel's third week the class was going on a five-night camping trip out to the country. But it turned out I didn't need to worry at all, as school became the place where Daniel was most at peace. To all our amazement, as Mom, Dad, and I waited by the school gate to welcome him home from the trip, he bounced down from the bus, laughing and joking in near-perfect Danish with a new friend.

Yet the joy of knowing that he was making friends and having fun at school was dampened by a conversation I had with his teacher soon after. I was waiting to collect him from school one afternoon when she asked me to step into the classroom while Daniel waited in the corridor outside.

"I'd like you to see this," she said, handing over a picture of tanks and dead bodies lying in the street, covered in blood. "He's been writing about it too," she added. "Maybe he needs some help?"

Later that night, when the lights in his room were low and Roksana was sound asleep, I sat down on the edge of his bed and asked him about the picture. Daniel hesitated at first, and turned away, but then he surprised me.

"Grandpa told me that we had to go and help Khanoum because some bad people had been fighting near her house. We went, and there was a house that was all broken because of a bomb. I saw dead bodies in the street too. There was a lot of blood."

We sat in silence. I knew about the bomb already, how the war against Iraq was no longer confined to the western border as it had been when Mohammad was alive. The Iraqis had started bombing the cities, and Isfahan had been hit a few months earlier. Dad said that the planes must have been aiming for the mosque, but they missed. The bombs had hit right on Farshadi Street, a few hundred feet away from Khanoum's home.

I sat and stroked his arm. It was Daniel who broke the silence. "I don't want to go back to Iran. The teachers there are bad men. They beat you if you get anything wrong. The teachers here don't do that. I want to stay."

That first conversation unlocked others. Over the coming days and weeks Daniel gradually revealed the truth about his life in Iran, stories that were even more shocking than the first. The more Daniel told me, the more I understood that the biggest threat to life back in my homeland was not the brutal war with Iraq, but the cruelty of the regime.

As much as I worried about what might happen in our home

if Daniel did stay, from everything he had told me, life in Iran was even more unpredictable and dangerous than it was here with Asghar in Denmark. And I think perhaps my parents knew this too. It was best for Daniel to stay, wasn't it?

———

A few days before they were due to return to Iran, my parents witnessed a scene that I feared would make them change their minds about leaving Daniel. I was working in the kitchen while the others were sitting in the living room watching TV one afternoon when Asghar and my dad got into an argument. I had no idea how it started, but I came into the room to see Asghar standing up, screaming at my father. Then Asghar picked Roksana up from the floor and hurled her toward the couch. She hit the wall above it and slid down to the cushions below. She cried, and I went to her as my dad yelled and left.

Dad did not come back for hours. Asghar disappeared, too, and I spent much of the time after both of them left feeling the fear rise within me. Was my dad okay? What would he say when he finally did return? Would the conflict between him and Asghar resume?

When at last there was a knock on the front door, I opened it to see Dad standing next to a stranger who had found him, lost and anxious on the street. I thanked the good Samaritan and ushered my dad inside.

Nursing a cup of sweet tea, Dad and I sat in silence at the table awhile. When he finally spoke, he only did so briefly about how angry Asghar had made him. "There are so many like him back home," he said. Then he tried to talk a little about life in

Iran. I listened, silently, but his words were halting, as if blocked somewhere deep in his chest.

Eventually he placed the cup carefully on the table and looked up at me. He sighed. "Daniel will be safer here with you."

———

As soon as I said good-bye to my parents at the airport, I started counting down the days until Asghar next exploded. He had already started to crack, with angry whispers in the middle of the night if Roksana wanted to sleep beside me. It didn't matter to him that, for the first year of her life, she had slept on my chest and now sleeping alone seemed unnatural to her. Asghar hated any show of affection toward the children, and I learned to wake up the instant either of them cried at night. If I didn't, he would go to them first, and their cries would only grow louder.

It was late in the afternoon the day Asghar's violence toward Daniel returned. A few days had passed since my parents had gone, and I was standing at the kitchen window, watching Daniel play outside with some friends.

I heard Asghar approach from behind. He leaned over, opened the window, and shouted down to the boys below. "Daniel, come!"

Daniel looked up and froze. He was fifty feet away, but I could see the terror on his face.

A minute later he was back inside, out of breath.

Asghar slapped him hard around the head. "Why didn't you ask me if you could go out?"

"Asghar," I said, trying to keep my voice calm. "It's all right. He did ask if he could go outside. I said it was okay as long as he stayed where I could see him."

Asghar turned to me, his body blocking Daniel in against the wall. He stared hard, his eyes cold. When he spoke he spat the words out as if they were poison. "But he didn't ask me."

I pushed past, trying to reach Daniel, who had started crying, but Asghar's arms were too long and too strong. He pushed me back, and I lost my footing. Daniel's crying only got louder as Asghar turned to him and shouted. "Your mother can't teach you how to behave properly, but I will!"

I scrambled along the floor to Daniel and wrestled him away before Asghar could hurt him again. Asghar spewed a sewer's worth of obscenities at us and slammed the door behind him as he left.

I kept my voice quiet as I tried to encourage Daniel to come away from the wall he was now curled up against. "It's okay. He's gone. It's okay, Daniel."

The trouble was, I didn't believe what I was saying. I was desperate inside. How could we cope if life was already like this just a few days after Mom and Dad had gone?

Four months earlier I had been feeling lost and aching with the pain of missing Daniel. Now I had a new nightmare playing out within me. I was terrified of what might happen if I ever left the kids alone with Asghar. I spent every moment thinking about Daniel and Roksana and how I could keep them safe. I knew that life at home in Iran was dangerous in so many ways and it was better to be here in Denmark, but would things ever really be okay?

HAVING SPENT MONTHS MARKING THE days on the wall in the Turkish jail, I continued to live my life by the clock in Denmark. Only, instead of counting days, I counted minutes.

If I was at college and the final lesson was in progress, I would know precisely how much time I had until I could spring up from my chair, sprint to collect Roksana from preschool, and then hurry back home before Daniel's bus would deliver him home.

If Daniel went to the bathroom at home and I couldn't see Asghar, I would only wait so long until I went and checked that my son was okay.

And if Asghar was raging, I would try and keep his anger directed at me long enough that Daniel and Roksana could run and hide in the cupboard under the sink.

I could never relax.

The only time I ever laughed was when I was with friends at college, but even then the happiness was short-lived. Within seconds I would be reminded of Asghar or worry about what might happen next when one of the children woke up. My chest would once again feel as though it was full of stones.

I was constantly worried about the children, and I couldn't eat more than a few mouthfuls of food before the nausea would take over. Adrenaline ran throughout my whole body constantly, robbing me of sleep, putting me in a state of constant high alert.

In the mornings, while Asghar slept, the children and I would eat in near-perfect silence. We used plastic cutlery instead of metal to minimize noise, and we whispered our conversations behind doors, which we had closed with gentle care.

Asghar often slept in late and went out in the afternoon, not returning until the early hours or the next day. On those precious afternoons when the house was our own, the contrast to our silent mornings was immense. There would be singing and laughing, music playing, and jokes cracking. But once the door handle turned and Asghar walked in, the spell would be cast. Winter would descend. All joy would vanish.

There were times when Asghar would be calm. Whenever he invited guests over he would often be the charming host, a perfect blend of warmth and wit. I knew that he wanted me to play along and pretend that all was well, and I did the best I could to smile and laugh when he joked. But for Daniel and Roksana, the unpredictability of it all only made things worse.

We were approaching the second anniversary of Daniel's arrival when Asghar informed me one day that he had invited some friends over to eat that night. By then, I had worked out how to make sure we didn't starve, in spite of the way money seemed to evaporate in Asghar's hands. Since I was the one who cashed the monthly welfare checks, I made a point to head straight to the store and load up on enough rice, tomatoes, and beans to last the next four weeks as soon as we had the money. But if, for some reason, Asghar found the money before I could get to the store, we learned to live without the luxuries and still survive.

The thing about this particular night, though, was that

Asghar had already taken the last of the money for the month. I looked in the kitchen cupboards and wondered what I could make out of the half dozen ingredients I found. I thought about asking Asghar for some cash to go buy some meat to maintain our façade in front of his friends, but then I stopped myself. Why was I doing all this? I was done pretending. If he wanted guests to come and eat with us, they'd have to eat like us.

When the couple arrived, we welcomed them in. I'd not met them before, but they seemed nice enough. They were Iranian, of course, and Asghar talked with the husband, a smartly dressed man named Soleyman, at length about politics. They filled the apartment with cigarette smoke and bragged to each other about how much they were doing to support the Shah and take down the regime. The wife—Sadaf—remained quiet throughout. I wondered if she was pretending too.

When Asghar waved his hand in the way that I knew meant he wished me to tidy the dishes away, I set to work. My arms were full of plates when Asghar pointed at an ashtray that was overflowing onto the table. "Clear this too," he said before reaching out for the bottle of whiskey that was rapidly going down.

"I'm busy," I said. "Can't you clear it?"

He snapped instantly. His chair flew back, and he swung his arm out toward my head, the bottle of whiskey just missing my eye as I ducked. The dishes crashed to the floor.

"What are you saying? You don't think I'm the man of the house? You clear it up!"

I tried to shout him down, but he was in my face, his hot breath a stench of booze and tobacco. His free hand pushed me back against the wall, the whiskey bottle poised above his head, ready for another shot.

He was a little drunk already, and as he lost his footing I slipped under his arm and back around the table. Sadaf and her husband sat in silence, both of them staring at Asghar. I didn't care that they were seeing it all. I was done trying to cover for him.

"I'm going to kill you!" Asghar waded through the chairs, and I ran to the bathroom. I heard our guests try to calm him down, and I strained to listen for sounds that would tell me whether the children were awake. They had heard these fights so often there were times that they just slept right through them.

Then I heard the front door slam. Footsteps approached the bathroom. After a gentle knock, I heard Sadaf's voice.

"Annahita, are you okay?"

"Has he gone?"

"Yes."

I unlocked the door. Sadaf reached for my hand. "Is this normal, what he did?"

I closed my eyes and nodded. I wanted to be free from all this hiding.

"Annahita, I can help you. I have a friend who works for Social. I know you're afraid, but you don't have to live like this."

I panicked. Social was the government department that kept us alive. They paid our rent and paid for our food. If Asghar knew that I was talking to them about him he would be even more enraged.

I begged her to say nothing. "Please, Sadaf, you must leave. I must clear up."

She did as I asked. I closed the front door behind her, once again hoping to hide the secret of Asghar's violence. I had been in this situation so many times already, wanting to let someone help me but terrified of what might happen if Asghar found out. Life couldn't carry on like this forever, could it?

Asghar was off on one of his trips one weekend, and I spent that Saturday morning looking through the classified section of the local newspaper and listening to Roksana and Daniel laugh out loud at the cartoons they were watching on television. My eyes rested on an advertisement for a cheap, small piano, and, on impulse, I phoned the number, visited the seller that afternoon, and knocked the bargain price down even lower.

The next day, the apartment was home to a squat little wooden piano. Its lacquer was chipped and the wood stained with coffee cup rings and cigarette burns, but it was mine. I carefully wiped clean the keys until they shone as best they could. I had never had any lessons and played no other instruments, but I loved simply the idea of being able to play, as well as the prospect of my children growing up in a house where they could make their own music. That felt like the kind of thing a good mother would do for her kids.

Of course, Asghar was dismissive of this when he finally came home on Sunday evening, but I ignored him. I practiced playing every day, trying to let my fingers become familiar with the keys and the different notes that hid behind them. I couldn't play any tunes that anyone would recognize, but if I let myself, I found that for just a few moments I would fall into the music. Everything else, for just a few seconds, would fade away.

A month after the piano arrived I came home with the children to see Asghar sitting around the apartment with a man I had not seen before, a strange-looking rug on the floor between them, and no piano. I spoke carefully as I took off my shoes.

"Where's my piano, Asghar?"

He didn't look at me, but smiled at his friend, put on his calm and gentle voice, and spread his hands wide like a politician. "I gave it away, Annahita. My friend here was in need of it."

I looked at the man he was taking to. He nodded and smiled back at Asghar.

"He was kind enough to give us this carpet," Asghar added.

I looked down. It was old, stained, and, the closer I looked, the more obvious it became that it was in fact made of two separate, equally old and shabby carpets sewn clumsily together. It was a joke of a carpet. It was almost funny.

But I wasn't laughing. Inside I felt such anger rise within me. I looked back at Asghar and his friend, grinning at each other like a pair of fools. "Why did you do that?" I spat.

"It is not your choice," Asghar said, his voice less cheerful now. "This is my life, my home, and these are my things. If I want to give anything within it to my friends, then I will."

"And get something like this in return?"

Asghar shot up, but then checked himself. His smile was gone, but something was different about him. He was holding back. I didn't stop to wonder why, but pointed back to the carpet. "Look," I said. "It's pathetic."

Asghar's friend stood up, coughed loudly, wished Asghar well, and headed for the door.

Once Asghar closed it behind him, he turned around and stared at me. Daniel and Roksana knew to be quiet and invisible whenever we walked in on Asghar, and they hadn't said a word since we got back. But as Asghar glared at me, they slipped out of the room and down the corridor toward the bathroom.

I was glad they didn't see Asghar pull the box cutter out of his pocket, or watch him as he marched toward me, turning over furniture, pulling at the blinds, destroying everything around him like a tornado.

I don't remember much after the first hit. I do remember being on the floor, desperately trying to kick him away. I remember the blade in his hand and him slashing at my feet. Nothing more.

I was in the hospital when I woke up. A nurse was checking the bandages around my foot. She tried to ask me some questions, but I said as little as I could. I was desperate to get home and make sure that the children weren't alone with Asghar for one minute longer than they had to be.

I returned home, and later that night, after I had put them both to bed and walked back on my crutches into the kitchen, Asghar stood in the doorway. "Why aren't you talking to me? You haven't said anything since you came back."

I kept my eyes down and started on the dishes.

"I helped you. It was me who called the ambulance, me who made sure that you were taken care of . . ." His voice trailed off. I kept my silence.

"Why are you not happy with me?"

I had done a lot of thinking that day. The usual thoughts and fears had been pressing down upon me—could I really put my family through the shame of losing another husband? How would I survive on my own with two children? If I stayed and Asghar put me in the hospital again, what would happen to the children? Back in Iran they'd be left alone, but here in Denmark Social was bound to take them away if they thought the kids were in danger.

I had kissed the Bible more than once by that time, sending up prayers for I-didn't-know-what to I-didn't-know-who.

I hadn't yet come up with a plan to get us away that I was convinced would work, but as I stood with my back to Asghar, watching his reflection in the window above the sink, I heard myself tell him that I wanted a divorce. Finally, after wanting to leave for so long but not being able to, I was ready. I had to do it. If I didn't get out, he wouldn't just end up killing me; the children's lives would be in danger too.

Asghar didn't hesitate with his reply. "No," he said quietly before walking out. "You either live with me or you die. That is the only choice you can make."

I decided to miss college the next day to begin planning our escape. After I said good-bye to Daniel and took Roksana to school, I picked up the phone and made some preliminary calls to start getting us out.

At some point, Asghar woke up, came out of the bedroom, and stood, arms crossed, watching me on the phone. While I was mid-sentence, he snatched the phone out of my hand, told me I was bluffing, and swore into the phone. "I don't care whichever of her friends you are. My wife's an idiot, and there's nothing you can do to help her."

Then he grabbed the handset with both hands, pulled the wires out of the wall, and marched to the nearest window, from which he hurled the whole phone.

"I'm going to kill you," he said, turning back toward me.

He didn't use the knife that morning, and he got tired quickly. When he stopped, I grabbed my bag and went to college. At least I would be safe there for a few hours. This time, I didn't bother to try to cover up the bruises or to disguise the fact that I could not lift my left arm away from my ribs. There didn't seem to be any point pretending anymore. I needed to escape, and the more people that knew it, the better.

Later that afternoon, I arrived home with Roksana and found Asghar waiting outside the apartment, a broad smile across his face, his arms held out wide for an embrace. "She's coming!" he said. "Next week. She's finally coming!"

"Who?"

"Cherie. We're all going to be together again, and we'll be happy. It's all going to be okay, Annahita."

His news threw me. Five years had passed since I last saw Cherie, and even though she was not my daughter, I had always felt a mother's love for her. If I left her alone with Asghar, would she really be okay? Could I trust him not to hurt his own child?

I couldn't think clearly. I was trapped beneath fear and confusion. One thing I was sure about, however, Asghar wasn't going to change. No matter how much he smiled and hugged and talked about the family getting back together, I knew his words were meaningless.

And I knew that Cherie needed me.

———

One night soon after Cherie arrived, she couldn't sleep. I jumped from my bed as soon as I saw her standing in our doorway and managed to get her back to her bedroom before Asghar woke up. She said she was upset and had had a bad dream, and as I lay down with her, she whispered about what life had been like with Ziynab in Iran. Cherie told me that she didn't like her at all, that she hurt her. "Everything is bad in Iran," she said. "Not like here."

Since Ziynab had come to Denmark with Cherie, it didn't take long to see that though Cherie was no longer in Iran, she had not escaped pain and fear. Ziynab was angry almost from the very start, and now her focus turned to Daniel.

"This is my son's home, so why is he here?" she'd say to me when he was at school. "Why did he have to come to Denmark? Why are you so soft with him? When are you going to learn how to be a good mother?"

After a few days, she started talking about me to Asghar while I was in the same room. "Your wife's a whore. You should divorce her."

"Why do you put up with her? A real man wouldn't accept it."

"You forget what women are like back in Iran. They don't disobey their husbands like she does."

Asghar's anger fed on her lies. He had always punished Daniel more readily than Roksana, but within a week of his mother's arrival he was slapping both Roksana and Cherie as well. The whole apartment regularly filled with shouting and tears as Asghar prowled and hit like a wounded bear.

I would try my best to protect the children, to give Asghar a different target to aim at. It worked most of the time, but the way he attacked me changed too. His box cutter came out of his pocket quicker, his fists moved faster, and while he used to stop when he grew tired, he seemed now to be driven by a new passion. More than once, I was sure he was finally about to kill me. And yet, somehow, he didn't.

Asghar's attacks on me created a special bond between Daniel, Cherie, and Roksana. Daniel learned to get them quickly to safety, scooping little Roksana up in his arms, placing his hands over her ears, and singing soft lullabies to her while Asghar cursed and screamed at me.

When each storm finally passed, I would go find them in the bathroom. The door would always be locked, and I would have to convince Daniel that it was me and that it was okay for him to open up.

———

"We are going to the Christmas party tonight," Asghar announced one evening as I cleared away the dishes. The children were playing in their room. "Soleyman has invited us, and you need to be ready in time."

Sadaf had become a good friend in the months since we'd first met, and any other time I would have been happy to go. But not now. I was tired of all the lies that were being told about me by Ziynab. I was exhausted by the weight of having to protect the children from a man whose heart was scarred with hatred and evil. I had struggled for so long, tried so hard to keep going, but I had nothing left anymore. Everything had grown dark. I could see no light in the world.

It was nothing new. Twice before I had felt this same way: the day I took the taxi to the court in Isfahan, hoping to get a divorce, and the cold morning in the mountains as I pulled Roksana's silent body from the rocks. I had wanted to end my life on both those occasions, but this was something different. This darkness was even more suffocating.

I knew that I had responsibilities, that my children depended on me. I could hear the voice within that said *how could I leave them?* but I did not feel strong enough to continue on. Asghar had said that he'd kill me, and I knew that one day he would. Sooner or later, my children would lose me.

The only power I had was this: I did not want to die at his hands. I wanted to die differently. I did not want to give my life to him. I wanted to take it myself.

"I don't want to go to the party," I said. "I'll stay behind."

"Are you surprised she doesn't want to go?" Ziynab said, her face souring as she drank her tea. "She doesn't want you to see her with her boyfriend."

I finished the dishes, laid the dishcloth on the side of the sink, and left the kitchen. She was still talking about me, calling me a whore and telling Asghar he was weak for letting me behave so scandalously, as I walked away.

I peeked in on the kids and breathed a final prayer for them. In the bathroom I reached up and pulled down the sleeping pills the doctor had given me. I hadn't taken many at all, since I hated the idea of not waking up whenever the children cried.

I walked to the bedroom, sat on the bed, and swallowed every last pill. Then I lay down.

———

It was Daniel who called the ambulance. I know that, because when I came around two days later, yet again in the hospital, there was an older lady standing by my bed, looking concerned and telling me everything that had happened since I last closed my eyes.

"You told the doctors about your husband. You said he beats you, that he's the one who caused all these injuries."

I was so tired, but somewhere inside I could feel myself panicking. It was like a scream coming from another room, gradually growing louder until it burst out of me.

"No!" I said. "Nothing's wrong at home. I just want to leave."

I knew they could see through my lie, but there was nothing they could do. I stuck to my story as other staff came in. Everything was fine. I had just felt depressed. I wanted to go home.

Asghar collected me from the hospital but didn't take me home straight away. He said that we needed to put things right, and that if I just sat back and closed my eyes I'd soon be back home with the children.

Everything was slightly blurred, and I was grateful for the chair he guided me to when we sat down at a desk in the bank. Asghar talked to the clerk about taking out a loan, a conversation I was only able to partly follow in my haziness. At some point I noticed the manager sitting beside me.

"Are you okay? You seem a little ill."

"I'm fine," I said. "Fine."

I lifted up the pen that Asghar had placed in my hand and signed the paper he guided me toward.

We left.

Once we finally got home, the warmth of the children as they cuddled in beside me on the bed sent me back off to my dreamless sleep.

⸻

I stopped going to college when Asghar's mother arrived, at least for the time being. It wasn't worth the taunts and abuse she threw at me whenever I got home. But my friends had not abandoned me. Sadaf visited me one day, and I told her why I had been taken to the hospital again and what had happened when I got out.

"What happened to the money you took out from the bank?" she asked.

"Asghar took it. He gave it straight to his mom."

She rolled her eyes. "How much?"

"About $2,000."

"That's crazy, Annahita. You can't live like this. You have to change something."

Up until that point, a part of me always thought I deserved this life. Even though I often kissed the Bible I hid on top of the bookcase and whispered desperate prayers, I couldn't escape the belief that God was angry and this was my punishment.

That afternoon, though, something about Sadaf's words struck home. Maybe things *could* be different.

"But how?" I asked.

"I want you to talk to my friend at Social."

I arranged to call Sadaf's friend from a pay phone one morning after I had said good-bye to the children. Even though I knew Asghar was nowhere nearby, I scanned the street for any sign of him.

"Annahita?" The woman's voice was unfamiliar to me. "Sadaf has told me about you. We want to help."

"How? He'll find out."

"No, Annahita. I promise that he won't find out. We can get you somewhere safe to stay. The children too."

"But you don't understand him. He'll find me and—"

"I know you're scared, but trust me when I say we can help you. All you need to do is call me when you're ready, and I'll tell you what to do."

I walked home quickly, not wanting to give Asghar any reason to be suspicious. Could I imagine myself calling the woman back and telling her I was ready to leave? That all seemed like a fantasy. But a nice one, nevertheless.

I got back to the apartment to find Ziynab making plans to return home at the weekend. She had been with us four months already, which, as she said, "was far too long to spend sharing a house with a whore for a daughter-in-law."

Asghar reminded her that she still had two months left on her visa, but her mind was made up. "I don't want to stay here a moment longer that I have to," she said.

I smiled inside. With Ziynab gone I might finally be able to get Social's help.

———

One afternoon when Daniel was playing with a friend and Ziynab had taken Cherie outside with Roksana to ride her new pink tricycle, Asghar launched another attack at me. Something had gotten into him again, and as his fingers closed tight around my neck I wondered for the hundredth time whether this would be the moment when he finally killed me.

I heard the front door open and Roksana call for me. I tried to reply, but Asghar's grip was so fierce no sound came out.

Asghar dragged me into the coat closet, jamming my back up against the wall and pulling the door almost closed.

"Mom?" cried Roksana. "Mom!"

Asghar stared into my eyes, both hands on me now. I couldn't breathe at all and was frantically scratching at his cheeks. I didn't want Roksana to see it end like this. I could see the blood on his cheeks, but nothing seemed to be stopping him.

The closet door opened. Roksana was standing there, her pink trike in one hand, her other held up to her face in horror. She opened her mouth wide to scream, but no sound came out.

Asghar let go. I pushed past him and picked up Roksana. She didn't stop trembling for the whole rest of the day. She did not speak. All day, all night she stayed the same, her body locked in silent terror.

She stayed like that for almost a week. I was terrified that she would never speak again.

———

I wish I could say that once I decided to take the woman from Social up on her offer that I had a surge of confidence or a sense that all would be well, but the truth is that when I waved good-bye to the children and walked to the pay phone the next morning, I still felt as though life was barely worth living. I still felt deeply worried about the impact that my leaving would have on my family back home. And I still thought that if any single part of the plan failed, Asghar would almost certainly kill me.

But in spite of all that, I dialed. And in spite of the way my heart raced and my mouth suddenly went dry, I was finally able to say the words that I had tried to say since the very first night of our marriage, seven years earlier.

"Annahita?" said the woman, her voice familiar this time.

"I want you to get us out."

AFTER I FINALLY MADE THE CALL TO Social, I couldn't concentrate. I worried that my fear would show, that Asghar or Ziynab would suspect something was wrong. Fortunately, between packing her bags and telling Asghar why he should discipline me more, Ziynab was too busy to pay me much attention.

Asghar drove us all to the airport early on Sunday morning to drop Ziynab off for her flight back to Iran. After her bags had been checked he returned to wait in the car, which he'd double-parked outside, telling me to make sure his mother knew where to go. As I watched her clear passport control and climb onto the escalator, she turned back to me. "Make sure you take care of Cherie."

"I will," said. Without thinking, I carried on. "Everywhere I go, I'll take her with me."

It took a moment for the meaning of my words to register with Ziynab. When they did, I had just enough time to see the look of complete shock on her face before she ascended up into the ceiling.

I was committed now. I was confident that she would not be able to use a payphone in the airport, since she had changed all her money into Iranian currency before she left us. But as soon as she got home, in forty-eight hours time, I knew she would call Asghar and warn him. If I wasn't away by then, he'd kill me for sure.

When we got back, I cleaned the apartment and tried to think of a way to smuggle the bare minimum of clothes out for the children. The next morning at seven I collected one outfit for each of us, threw them in a trash bag, and opened the front door.

"Where are you going?"

I froze. Asghar never got up early. "I'm taking the garbage out. Did I wake you? I'm sorry."

He grunted and went into the kitchen. I didn't want to leave the children in the apartment with him awake, if even for a few minutes, but if I didn't go down to the dumpsters, he'd surely be suspicious.

I ran down the stairs as fast as I could, hid the bag down the back of the bin, and rushed back to the apartment, checking on the children as soon as I returned. They were eating in silence, just as they had been when I left. Asghar had gone back to bed.

I breathed a sigh of relief and bundled the children into the car for school. They all attended the same one, and the car was full of happy chatter as I drove them, following the tracks that had been cut into the February snow by other motorists. Ziynab's departure had put all of them in a good mood.

As soon as I said good-bye to them at 8:30 a.m., I doubled back to the apartment block, pulled out the bag of clothes, and got back into my little beige Lada. There was no way Asghar could see me from the apartment block, but my nerves were so frayed that my hands fumbled the key in the ignition when I got back in. I pulled away, checking my mirrors for any last-minute sight of Asghar running after me. All I saw was snow and parked cars.

I made my way to my college and phoned social services as

they had instructed me to do. They gave me the address of a safe house thirty minutes' drive away. I went back to the car and checked the fuel gauge. I could go forty miles, max. I prayed it would be enough. I had $15 in my purse, but I had other plans for that money.

I sat in the parking lot, a piece of paper on my lap and a pen in my hand. I thought of all the things I wanted to say to Asghar. I wanted him to know how much he had hurt me, how much pain he had caused the children, how great the suffering he had inflicted on us all. I wanted to rage at him, but there was no time for that. Instead I put down everything I wanted to say in the simplest possible form.

Asghar,

I am leaving you. You can never, never see me again. I am never coming back to you.

Annahita

It was past 9 a.m. now, and I knew I had to move quickly. Asghar would expect me back with the children from school at 2 p.m. When we didn't show he'd come searching for us. He always did, and I didn't want him to visit the school or my college in one of his violent moods.

I caught a friend who was about to go into class. "Can you deliver this to Asghar at two today?"

"Give it to Asghar?" she said. "No way! He'll kill me."

I knew she was right, so I drove to the post office, filled out my address on the envelope, and asked the lady at the counter to deliver the letter that afternoon.

"Honey, this place is so close you can deliver it yourself."

"Oh, no," I said, trying to smile. "It's a surprise, and I can't be the one to deliver it. But it has to get there at two, no earlier, okay?"

It cost me $6, but it was worth every bit of it.

At 10:05 a.m. I was in a drugstore buying toothbrushes and paste.

At 10:23 a.m. I was back at the children's school, parking the car on a side street. When I told the teacher that I needed to take Daniel, Cherie, and Roksana out, she nodded. "Of course," she said. She looked at me for a moment. "You're not coming back, are you?"

"No," I said.

She smiled. "Take care of them."

At 10:35 a.m. we were all in the car, engine running, windows steamed. I turned round and looked at them. They looked confused.

"I want to divorce Asghar," I said. "I'm never going back to him. If you want to come with me you can. If you don't, you can go back to school and stay with him. It's up to you."

Six little eyes darted back and forth between each other. Then, like sunrise on a winter's morning, three giant smiles rose on their faces. "Yay!" they shouted, arms waving, car rocking. "We're free!"

There was so much snow on the freeway as we drove that the thirty-minute journey took over an hour. I was gripping the wheel, staring hard and wiping the condensation off the windshield. It was only when we reached the town that I realized I had no map with me, and I hadn't even written the address of the safe house down. It was almost noon, and I had no idea how I was going to find the place.

"Liljehaven . . . Liljehaven . . ." I repeated the name of the street over and over, looking up at the road signs, feeling my breathing get even tighter. I didn't want to do it, but I knew I needed to ask for directions. Only when I saw a couple of women walking into a shop ahead did I decide to pull over.

At 12:13 p.m. I parked the car and looked up at the street name. Liljehaven.

Five minutes later we had pulled in front of the house through tall metal gates and parked the car in the garage, the doors quickly closing behind.

Once we had been shown the bedroom we would all sleep in and the children had been introduced to some others playing quietly in a lounge, I sat in the office with a woman who said her name was Anna. "Can you tell me your story?" she asked.

It took hours. I told her everything. There was no detail I left out, no part of the story that I kept hidden. For the very first time since Asghar took me to the bedroom on the night of our wedding to earlier today when I left him, I shared my story.

When I finished, Anna was silent. I felt drained, exhausted, but lighter as well.

I looked at my watch. It was 2:30 p.m. By now he would know. I pictured him, a wild animal loose in the apartment, running about the streets in search of us, his hand clenched around his box cutter.

The terror returned, and I felt like I couldn't breathe again.

It was the next day that I heard what Asghar had done. As soon as he opened the letter he phoned the police. He told them how worried he was because his beloved wife and three precious children had not yet returned from school. He was scared that something had happened to them, and could the police do something to help, anything at all?

He dropped the act when he phoned my friends. He swore and threatened and told them that if they didn't tell him where I was, he'd come round and cut them up.

And then he went to Social. I don't know how he knew they were involved, but he knew it. He told them he was going to burn the building down with all of them still inside. He pushed furniture around, told them that it was all their fault, and said they were trying to take his wife and children away. He said that everything I had told them in the hospital was a lie and they were idiots for believing even a single word of it.

Anna told me all of this as we sat in the office. She had to keep on reassuring me that I was safe, that there was no way he would find out where we were. I had to wrestle with my thoughts to believe her.

"But there's one problem," she said. "Cherie's not your daughter. Until you divorce Asghar and get custody of her, he has every right to go to the police. If he does, you'll have to let us take her back to him."

The thought terrified me almost as much as I knew it would terrify Cherie.

———

For days we didn't hear anything from Asghar or the police. I was sure that he'd try to get Cherie back, and his silence confused me. It was only when Anna received a call from Social that I knew what was going on.

"Asghar is sick," she said. "He's been taken to the hospital, but I don't know what's wrong. They say he's not going to be home for at least a few days. Do you want to go back and get the rest of your things?"

We only had the one change of clothes each and no money to buy anything else that we needed. I told Anna that I wanted to go back but only if someone would go with me.

I called a friend and asked her husband, Reza, to meet me at the apartment the next night at 9 p.m.

It was dark when I pulled up and saw him waiting on the street. I believed that Social was right when they said Asghar wasn't at home, and I knew that Reza was a man I could trust, but I still had to fight the urge to turn around and flee.

We drove around the block and saw that the apartment was dark. I asked Reza to go in first and that I would come up once the lights were on.

"I don't know why, but I don't feel like it's safe. Would you mind?" I said.

"You know he's not there, Annahita. I just spoke to him in the hospital two hours ago. It's going to be fine to go up there."

"You spoke to him? Do you know what he's sick with?"

"He said he had blood in his urine. He'll be fine, but they're keeping him in for observations."

I handed over the key and watched Reza cross the road. Two minutes later the light in the apartment lounge went on. I told myself not to be scared, stepped out of the car, and followed Reza's snowy footprints.

As soon as I reached the doorway at the top of the stairs, I stopped. I could hear voices. Both of them were familiar. Reza's I could place, but the other—a woman's—had me confused for a second.

It was Ziynab.

I stepped back and pinned myself to the wall. It had been nine days since I'd seen her off at the airport, a week since Asghar had read my note. She still had two months on her visa, and I guessed Asghar must have called her as soon as he found out I'd gone. And there she was, sitting in the apartment with the lights out while her son was in hospital. She must have been waiting for me. I had never felt more scared of her.

"So, where's Asghar?" Reza was trying to sound calm, but failing.

Ziynab sounded too nice when she spoke. "In the hospital. He could do with some cigarettes. Could you take him some?"

"Sure."

"And can you take me too?"

"Yes!" said Reza, his voice unnaturally loud and slow. "Of course I can take you to see Asghar."

I backed down the stairs and ran to the car. I killed my lights and drove far enough away so that I could just see Reza when he came out. He was alone, and I flashed him over.

"I told her I was going to buy some cigarettes and that I'd come back," he said as soon as he got in. "We should go."

———

A few days later, I was back at the apartment. This time it was daylight, and instead of Reza by my side I had three police officers, two male and one female. Anna had told them about Ziynab and Asghar, and they had agreed to help me get whatever I needed. Still, no matter how many times they told me that it was all going to be fine and that I could relax, my heart still threatened to beat its way out of my chest.

"What do you want?" Ziynab shouted through the locked door.

"We're here to recover some property," said one of the officers. "Open up now."

"I can't find the key. I can't open the door. I'm sorry, Officer."

"Yes, you can. If you don't unbolt the door, we'll break it down."

The door opened, and Ziynab looked at the police with disdain. When her eyes landed on me, her expression momentarily changed to disgust.

Then she quickly switched back to mock innocence. "I'm a guest here. I can't let you in."

The officers were getting impatient now. "Yes, you can. This apartment belongs to this lady here, and we're going to let her get whatever items she wants."

She started swearing at them in Farsi, calling them all kinds of terrible things. All of the officers were Danish, but they understood the tone well enough.

"Be quiet and sit down," they said, escorting her to her bedroom and blocking the door.

"Okay, Annahita" said the female officer, pulling out some garbage bags from her pocket. "Tell us what you want."

I was shaking so hard it was almost impossible to think.

"It's all yours, remember. You can take it. It's okay."

I couldn't speak, I was so nervous. I pointed out a few clothes and some toys.

"You want the television?"

I nodded. I didn't think to look for any papers or photos. I just wanted to get out of there as soon as I could. We filled the bags and then quickly left to return to the safe house. When I walked back in through the doors, I breathed a prayer of thanks. We'd actually made it back.

———

The first I knew that Asghar was out of hospital was when Anna rushed into my room at the safe house one morning a fortnight later. Daniel, Cherie, and Roksana were at their new school, and I was doing chores.

"You need to come," she said. "The school's office is calling. Asghar's there."

Visions flashed through my mind of him holding the children hostage, waving his box cutter in the air. It was only when I spoke to the secretary that I understood that the children were safe.

"He was at the main gate during recess, and your son saw him from out the window and told us about him. None of your children went outside; they're all safe here in the office. But it's best if you come and get them now."

It turned out there had been an error in the school administration system, and because they didn't have our address at the safe house, Asghar had been sent the details of the upcoming parent-teacher conference instead.

Anna and I went to the school and got the children safely home, but the episode marked the end of their time at school—as well as the end of any of us going out beyond the tall metal gates. From then on, they were taught in our room by a string of visiting teachers. I was so grateful for their kindness, but couldn't help feeling that I had become a prisoner once again.

Asghar was obviously well recovered from his illness by then, so it wasn't surprising that he proceeded to contact the police and tell them I had kidnapped Cherie. Receiving the court summons made me glad I'd had divorce papers drawn up in the meantime. If he was going to take Cherie against her will, I was going to fight to get her back.

———

When I walked into the courtroom, it was the first time I had seen him in six months.

He looked old.

But as he stared hard right into my eyes, I knew he was ready to fight.

I listened to him explain to the judge how he had done nothing wrong, and that after a few arguments at home, I had decided to punish him by taking his daughter away from him, against his will. He was every bit as charming as I knew he could be, and for a moment I thought the judge might just believe him.

"I didn't kidnap Cherie," I said. "I was so afraid of him, and he was so angry that I thought the only way to protect her and the others was to get away."

Someone from Social stood up and explained about how they were helping us and why they thought we were at risk. The judge listened carefully and delivered his verdict. I had a simple choice to make: I could either give Cherie back, or I could spend six months in jail and have all of the children taken away from me. Either way, Cherie was going back to Asghar.

What choice did I have? Asghar had won again. I promised

to let Cherie return to her father, feeling sick inside at the thought of all the fear and pain she would endure as a result.

As I walked out of the courtroom with Anna, I kept my eyes away from Asghar, only daring to look out the back of the car as Anna paused at the gates at the front of the courtyard. Asghar was coming up behind us, driving a little white Toyota. In the passenger seat was Ziynab. Both of them were looking our way. She was shouting.

The guards let us out, but as I looked back I saw they'd stopped Asghar from following.

———

Back at the safe house, I took Cherie to the laundry room, searching for somewhere quiet to break the news. "You know I'm not your biological mom, don't you?"

She nodded.

"I can't keep you. I'm not allowed. You have to go back to be with your dad."

Her shout was loud enough to shatter glass. In her anger I saw some of Asghar. But hers was not cruel or vicious. She was simply terrified and hated the injustice of it all. She was soon crying, telling me she didn't want to go, pleading between her sobs to be allowed to stay.

Immediately I was back in Isfahan, watching Daniel's form grow smaller and smaller through the car window. In that instant, one of my deepest wounds opened up inside, and I gathered Cherie in my arms and wept with her.

The court had given me two days to get Cherie back to her father, two days in which Cherie begged me not to make her go.

Roksana joined in, telling me that she would take Cherie's place. "Cherie can't fight so good," she reasoned. "But I can fight him. I won't let him hurt me."

In the end, I stopped trying to get Cherie not to cry. We were all sobbing as the taxi came and the person from Social loaded Cherie's bag into the trunk.

Daniel, Roksana, and I watched the car disappear, then closed ourselves in behind the gates. It was one of the worst days I had ever known.

Three days later Social phoned.

"He doesn't want her after all. He said Cherie hasn't stopped crying, won't sleep, and won't eat. He can't cope, nor can his mother. He says you can have her back."

———

Asghar wasn't the only Iranian in trouble with the Danish police. Once Cherie was returned to us in the safe house, a story hit the national news about an Iranian man killing his wife with a knife. Anna was far more bothered by it than I was. I had spent years listening to Asghar threatening to kill me, and my body had more than enough scars on it to testify to his fondness for knives. But still she encouraged me to do what I could to get Asghar to finally sign the divorce papers and put some distance between us.

I phoned Asghar to discuss it. He stayed quiet for much of the call, and I had to fight the urge to fill the space with my own words.

Eventually, after asking him to sign the papers for a third time, he spoke. "If you let me include Cherie and Roksana on my passport I will agree to a divorce." Since Denmark didn't require children to have their own passports, adding them onto Asghar's would give them the ability to travel outside the country with him. This was not something I wanted to consider.

"Why would you want that? You already know that Cherie doesn't want to live with you. How do you think she'd react if you took her to Iran?"

"Annahita, you know that I know where you live. And you know that if I want I can just take them from the street. You can't keep my children from me. So let's keep this friendly, shall we?"

Was he bluffing about knowing where we lived? I couldn't be sure, but I knew that he wasn't lying about the possibility of him snatching them as they walked. Daniel was ten now, Cherie nine, and Roksana six. I couldn't keep them in my sight all the time. And even if I was with them when he found us, I knew Asghar was stronger than me and would stop at nothing if his anger burned hot enough. The only thing to do was to secure this divorce. We could figure out the rest later.

So I said yes.

I drew up a letter detailing the agreement and took it, as Asghar instructed me, to the police station opposite the apartment. It was ironic that all the years I had spent being beaten, abused, and cut by Asghar in that home, the police had been just fifty feet away on the other side of the street. Never once had I called on them for help, yet now Asghar had found a way of getting them to do his dirty work.

"The police know about you taking Cherie from me," Asghar had said. "I have been talking to them about how much she means to me. If you take them the letter and the passports it'll help them understand that you're not a threat to the girls."

I parked out at the front of the station and walked straight in without looking up behind me at the apartment. I handed over the letter and left as quickly as I could.

Back at the safe house, Anna was appalled when I told her what I had done. "How could you do that? Don't you realize that he can leave the country at any time with them now? You've got to go and get it all back."

She was right. I knew that I had not acted wisely, and I felt bad for once again giving in to Asghar. I feared him so much that he had a strange power over me. I had spent so many years acting as his puppet it was hard to break the spell. But I was done with living in fear.

The next morning I made the short drive back. I pulled up out front, but then thought better of getting out of the car in daylight. So I parked in the lot around the back and went in the rear doors.

"I want to take the letter and passports back that I brought in last night."

"I'm sorry," said the officer on duty. "You're too late. You just missed your husband by a minute."

I knew that Asghar must have been watching me as I pulled up. "Which way did he go?"

The officer pointed to the front door. I turned to leave, but stopped. What if he was outside waiting for me? I felt hunted.

"Please," I asked. "Would you have someone escort me to my car? I'm scared."

The officer talked to me gently as we walked outside. He told me that I was safe and that he was sure that everything would get resolved quickly.

I locked the door as soon as I was in my car.

Just like the time when I went to the apartment with Reza, I knew something was wrong.

I held my breath and waited. I was sure Asghar was nearby, that he was watching me.

I started the engine and pulled away out of the lot and onto the road. It was early, just after seven, and there was hardly any traffic around as I made the next couple of turns.

As soon as I spotted the little white Toyota in my rearview mirror, I knew I was right. It was him, pushing up close behind me, close enough that I could see his face. He wanted me to know that he was stalking me.

I tried speeding up, but he maintained the same twenty-foot gap between us. I slowed down a lot, and still he kept the gap.

I made a sharp right turn; he stuck right with me. A left, he was still there.

What do I do now? How do I get away? I tried to reason it out, to find a way of getting clear of him, but my thoughts were frayed. Getting back to the police station would be good, but as I turned down side street after side street, I realized I had no idea where I was.

I hit a stretch of wide, straight road and accelerated hard. Asghar was still behind me, like I was towing him. I pushed the Lada as hard as I could, feeling the engine strain through the steering wheel. Asghar was even closer now, his windshield and the white hood of his car filling my rearview mirror. My thoughts took shape again, breaking through the adrenaline. If we carried on much longer one of us was going to get hurt. Perhaps one of us would die. Maybe we both would.

I slammed on the brakes, forcing my foot down as hard as I possibly could. I braced myself and waited.

The force and sound of the impact winded me, leaving me stunned for a moment. But my car was still running, and I put it back in gear and tried to pull away. I could feel the strain and hear metal tear against metal, but I made it.

I looked in my mirror to see Asghar standing on the street beside his car. It was a wreck, a mass of crumpled metal, twisted wheels and billowing smoke. There was no way he could follow me.

I'd not gotten farther than a couple of hundred feet when my ears rang out with the sound of sirens. A police car pulled me over.

"Stay here," said the officer when I stopped. "You're safe now."

I sat, engine off, shivering. I didn't want to drive any more, but I didn't want to be anywhere near Asghar either. I looked back and saw him, pinned against his wreckage by two other officers before being led into a squad car.

"That was quite some driving," said the officer once Asghar had gone. "Where did you learn? Hollywood?"

SOME GOOD THINGS CAME OUT OF THE car crash. The police took a more active role in keeping us safe from Asghar, and I suspect that they might have helped persuade him to sign the divorce papers too. They suggested we move from the safe house and even managed to persuade us to go back and live in the apartment. But even though they changed the locks and promised to be at the door within a minute if I called them, our time at home only lasted a couple of weeks. Asghar just couldn't keep away.

Eventually, we moved to a new safe house and tried to start over. The children began recovering from all that had happened. I tried to shield them as best I could, and for much of the time, I felt as though they were able to enjoy life. As we approached our first Christmas since leaving Asghar, they filled the air with excited chatter about presents, food, and all the things they were going to do during the school vacation.

All those plans changed when two police officers visited one afternoon. They told me that Asghar was planning on kidnapping the girls within the next twenty-four hours and that we should get as far away as possible as soon as we could.

I didn't know what to say. They insisted that they were taking the threat seriously and told me to phone my friends to see if I could stay with some of them for the Christmas vacation.

"You've got three hours." I knew most of the police from the station by now, and one of them was the same female officer who had accompanied me on the first visit back to the apartment when Ziynab had hurled Farsi obscenities while the officer collected my things for me. "Don't worry," she added as she stood in the doorway, about to leave. "It's going to be okay. You've got an angel on your shoulder."

Her words caught me.

Ever since I had been given the Farsi Bible, I had picked it up and prayed from time to time. The worse Asghar's attacks had gotten, the more I had prayed. I found that it helped, much like drinking a glass of cool water took away the dryness in my mouth on a hot night. To my mind, prayer was like medicine, only to be taken in the most extreme of times.

But an angel on my shoulder? That sounded different, and unlike anything I had ever learned in a mosque. There, it was all about fear and rules and the difficulty of earning a route to paradise. I had never thought of God being interested in helping me before, let alone being with me all the time. I liked the idea. It gave me courage.

———

Three hours later the police returned to find our bags packed and the children and me ready to go. "Where to?" they asked.

"Sweden."

It only took us an hour to get through Copenhagen, cross the bridge that took us to Sweden, and reach the city of Malmo, but having an international border separating us from Asghar made me feel a little safer.

We stayed with Iranian friends for the whole of the vacation. I had brought the Bible with me, and just about every day I brought it out to hold and kiss. I knew I was praying to Jesus, though I had no real idea who he was. I simply knew without doubt that it was helping.

My friends and I talked a lot during the time we spent together. We talked about where I might take the children to live. Canada sounded nice. Then again, Sweden appealed too. The culture was similar to Denmark's, the country was ten times bigger, and the children and I could understand the language already. If I was going to start a new life in a new country as a single mother, I wanted to make things as simple as possible.

There was another reason to choose Sweden. I knew I would not be allowed to take Cherie with me, wherever I went. Though Asghar had given Cherie back to me three days after the court had granted him custody, technically, he was still her legal guardian. The police had let me bring her to Malmo, but only on the understanding that I would return with her as planned in the new year. If I left the country for good, I would have to return her to her father. And if I was forced to leave her with Asghar, the thought of us being thousands of miles and a whole ocean apart felt wrong.

Once Christmas break was over, we only went back to Denmark for a few days. The police were clear that Asghar was still a threat, and they wanted me to get away as quickly as I could, which meant saying good-bye to Cherie and letting Social take her back to live with Asghar.

It was no easier the second time than it had been the first. The words caught in my throat and the tears stung my eyes. "We will see each other again soon," I said, finally, hoping that I was right.

———

Our second stay in Malmo felt different than the first. Though we had only been gone a few days, it was as if the air had changed. At Christmas I had felt as though there were some options that might be forming in the mist ahead of us, but as we returned I suddenly felt the need to be constantly looking over my shoulder.

Every time I saw a small white car I'd have two opposing instincts. Part of me wanted to make myself invisible and watch to make sure that it wasn't Asghar. Part of me wanted to grab Daniel's and Roksana's hands and run for our lives.

The weight of poverty was heavy as well. Just like our time in Istanbul I was starting over completely. I had nothing beyond the little cash I carried in my purse. I had no bank account and no permit to work. I applied to emigrate officially but was turned down the first time. I tried again, and still no success.

I had met a fellow Iranian named Siavash over Christmas break, who offered to help us out now, letting us have a couple of rooms in his new apartment up north. I had been wary when he admitted he knew Asghar, but as I got to know him, I relaxed a little. My friends who I'd stayed with trusted him and said he was dependable and honest. I still had my doubts, but I could see the sense in putting a few hundred more miles between us and Asghar. But how to afford it? To my surprise, Social back in Denmark phoned me and offered to pay my rent for the next year and a half. Maybe the angel was still on my shoulder after all.

By the time the support from Denmark came to an end, life was starting to settle. I no longer panicked when I saw a white car, and I had almost disciplined myself not to imagine the worst every time the phone rang. The apartment we lived in was on the same block as the school Daniel and Roksana attended, and whenever I was studying at home instead of going in to college, I would crack open a window and smile as I listened to the shouts of happy children floating up from below during recess.

Siavash and I, after many months of being friends, had started a relationship too. He was quiet and kind, and he didn't mind the way that the apartment would fill with noise when Daniel and Roksana came home from school, bringing their friends with them.

There were some old wounds that still hurt. I missed Cherie, and so did Roksana and Daniel. There were days when they grew frustrated at me for continually reminding them how important it was not to tell anyone about our past life in Denmark. Money was tight, and even though my immigration application had been accepted, I still had moments when I felt as though I was too many lifetimes away from the land in which I belonged.

But these problems were not nearly as large as the ones I had once had. Life—for the first time since the year that Mohammad and I had spent together—was finally beginning to be good again.

Then, two years after we left Denmark, Asghar found us. I don't know how long he had been searching or how he found us, but as I listened to the nightmarishly familiar phone call from the school secretary telling me that Asghar was in the building and was refusing to leave, I felt all the peace and happiness that had been forming within me evaporate in an instant.

I said nothing for a while. I could hear Asghar shouting in the background, cursing the staff and threatening to burn the school if they didn't bring out his daughter.

"Can you hear me? Are you there?"

I snapped back into the conversation. "What do I need to do?"

"The police are coming. I'll make sure they walk Daniel and Roksana back to you as soon as they can."

I held my composure long enough to tell her to be careful and say good-bye, and then I slid to the floor and sobbed.

Siavash arrived soon after the police brought Daniel and Roksana home. We all listened as they told us we had no option but to move.

"You mean to a safe house?" I asked.

"No, that's not possible. We need a better long-term plan, but for now there's a convent an hour away. You'll be safe there."

By 9 p.m. the four of us were standing in the courtyard of a tall, wide building, watching as a nun in gray robes approached. The air was still. "We'll be okay," I said out loud, as much for myself as for the children.

———

I woke up to a sound I could not describe. Roksana, Daniel, and Siavash were all asleep, and it was still dark outside. I wondered if I was maybe still dreaming, but the noise kept coming, drifting in through the cracks in the closed door.

I put on a sweater and followed the sound. Female voices rose and fell, like waves on a pebble beach. I hadn't taken much notice of the corridor on the way to our room the night before, but as I creaked my way along dark wooden floorboards, every few steps I passed a picture. The golds, reds, and deep blues shone from the white walls. I recognized the woman depicted in the picture as Mary, and the baby I guessed was Jesus, who, at the time, I still thought of as a prophet. As for all the other characters, they were lost on me.

Then I found the source of the noise. On the other side of a half-open door were twenty or thirty women, all dressed in the same gray clothes I had seen the night before. I backed away from the door and sat on a wooden chair in the corridor outside.

I knew they were praying, but the way they were praying was like nothing I had ever experienced before. In the mosque with Khanoum, prayer had bored me with its hollow words to a God who never replied. Ever since I had been given the Bible, my own prayers had been frantic, desperate pleas for help from someone I wasn't even sure liked me.

But these women and their prayers were different.

I couldn't understand the language, but the sound was beautiful. It was gentle and kind, and as I sat and listened I could feel my breath grow heavy within me. The fear that I had carried with me since the previous afternoon lifted. As it did, I felt calmer. It was as if I was listening with the very deepest part of myself. The longer I sat there, the more hungry I became to hear more. The more I heard, the more I wanted to join in. But I didn't know how or even what it was that was stirring within me, so I just listened. Eventually I padded my way back to my room, the women's prayers echoing inside me.

———

From the window in the corridor outside our room we could see a lake so large that its farthest shores were hidden beneath the horizon. I spent hours down by the water, and Daniel and Roksana didn't grow tired of being taken to the gift shop to look at the postcards they sold there. They sold homgrown produce, too, and since it was the time of year the nuns made apple jam, the corridors would fill up in the afternoons with the most delicious, sweet aroma.

The nuns were friendly and put up with me asking them questions about how they made the jam and who was who in the paintings.

Eventually, I summoned the courage to ask the question that I really wanted the answer to.

"What is it about this life that keeps you here?"

The nun I had chosen to ask was one of the oldest ones. Sister Elisabeth smiled and invited me to join her outside.

The air was cold outside. I liked the way that every time I inhaled it made my head feel just that little bit clearer. We stood on the terrace and looked out at the water. She didn't speak. She just looked out, smiling.

"I love God," she said eventually. "I want to give my life to serve him."

She looked at me, still smiling. That same heaviness of breath that I had experienced on the first morning returned. I wasn't just aware of the cold air around me; I felt like I was aware of everything. The world seemed more alive in that moment, as if I had pulled back a veil that had been covering me all my life.

Sister Elisabeth didn't say anything else, but carried on

looking at me. Her words echoed within me. Somewhere inside me I could feel something waking up, a sense that what I had just heard had the power to give me life.

I shivered. A different voice spoke within me. What did this old nun mean anyway? Everything I had learned about serving God in the mosque had always involved serving the mullahs, and those men were cruel and not to be trusted.

Could I really trust God the way that she did? Could I hope to find the kind of peace that lived within her? After so many years of giving up on God, could it be that he had not given up on me?

Sister Elisabeth's smile grew wider. Without saying anything she patted my arm and turned to go back inside. I stayed awhile. The stillness was something I didn't want to break.

A man and a woman from Social visited us after we had been in the convent a week. They spread a map of Stockholm on the bed. "You see these areas?" the man said, pointing to several different places on the map. "There are a lot of Iranians living here. A lot of foreigners too. You can't go there. But this place," he said, pointing to a town a ways outside the city, "this is fine. Nobody will know you here. Okay?"

"I guess," I said, looking at Siavash, who shrugged in return.

"But you're going to need new IDs. That means starting over, going into hiding, and never telling anyone about your old life. If we come back in an hour, can you tell us your decision?"

Daniel and Roksana agreed quickly. For Siavash, it was different. As far as anyone knew, he was in no danger from Asghar.

He could walk away from the convent, go back to the apartment, and carry on his life just as it had been before.

Or he could throw his lot in with us—three refugees with a psychopath of an ex-husband chasing after them.

He chose to stay with us.

And I got ready for a brand-new life.

THE TEN DAYS THAT WE SPENT AT THE convent were among the most beautiful that I can remember. I was scared some of the time, but there was a moment every day when that fear would fade so far into the background that I could almost forget it had ever existed. As I rose early, left the room while the others slept, and let the sound of the nuns praying pull me along the corridors, I would feel a sense of excitement rise within me. And as I sat on the chair and let my own prayers fall in whispers from my lips, I knew that I wanted to trust this God I was praying to.

The nuns prayed long and flowing prayers, but mine were stuttering, simple things. I asked God to help me. That was about it. And when I was done asking, I let my thoughts drift wherever they wanted. But still, I continued these faltering prayers, feeling a sense of peace warm me despite their simplicity.

Eventually, we moved from the convent to the town Social had suggested on the outskirts of Stockholm. For what felt like the hundredth time, the children enrolled in a new school and I signed up for a bunch of courses at a new college. The police had warned us not to contact any other Iranians, never to show any of our family photos to other people, and not to tell anyone anything about our life before. I reminded Daniel and Roksana of all this daily, but at twelve and eight, they were still just children. Roksana couldn't understand why I was so worried, and we fought all the usual battles that children and parents fight at that age. Only, for us, things weren't normal.

I knew I couldn't control what Daniel and Roksana said away from me any more than I could protect them as they walked home from school. Asghar had found us twice already, and I carried with me a constant, gnawing fear that he would do so again.

I missed Cherie too. Stealing away, moving to a new city, and keeping it all from her felt like a betrayal. I knew that if life had taught me anything, it was that it is full of hard decisions that often get harder the more we put them off. Even so, I was tired of shouldering so many burdens all the time.

Most of all, I felt more cut off than ever from my family back in Iran, and although I still spoke to my parents on the phone, I knew that my divorce from Asghar had been every bit as toxic for them as I had feared. The more I had suffered, the less I had been able to tell them. Added to that, it had been months since I had talked with Khanoum. The distance between me and my family felt greater with every passing year.

—

The news that Khanoum had suffered two heart attacks and was dying caught me off guard. It winded me just as severely as one of Asghar's punches to the stomach, and I struggled to concentrate or think clearly for hours after I finished the phone call with my aunt.

All I could think about was the last time I had seen my grandmother. It was the night I had found out that I had to choose which of my two children to leave behind in Isfahan. I was standing by the bed, staring at the piles of their little clothes, feeling sick at the thought of choosing just one to take with me.

Khanoum walked in. I hadn't known she was in the house. She hugged me, saying nothing. I wanted to hold onto her forever. I wanted to tell her everything about Asghar and the trouble he was in and the terrible choice I had to make. But I knew I couldn't. So I just kept on hugging her, holding her close so that she wouldn't look at me and see me break down and weep.

"I promise I won't die before you come back," she whispered. "I'll be waiting for you."

Hearing that she was dying set off a fire within me. I had to go back and see her. There was no option, no discussion, no possibility of any other solution. I had to go back. I had to see her while she was still alive.

I started making plans to visit Iran. The more I investigated what it would involve, the more complicated I understood the situation to be. Since I had not been living in Sweden for three years, there was a chance that my leaving the country might threaten my status as a temporary resident.

I needed a visa too. That meant going in person to the Iranian embassy in Stockholm. I would have to do all I could to hide the truth from them about why I had left Iran a decade earlier. If they saw through my story they could try to have me arrested, or worse.

And what about Daniel and Roksana? The thought of leaving them behind for the week that I planned to be away was painful in the extreme, but could I keep them safe there as well? At fourteen years old, Daniel was close to the age at which the regime drafted all boys into the army. If he came with me, I might lose him all over again.

Siavash presented the solution to the first problem. "We could get married," he said one evening as I agonized over it all.

"What?"

"We could get married. That way you could get a Swedish passport, and you'd be able to get back in the country."

What he said made sense. We had been together for over two years, and I knew Siavash to be a kind and gentle man who took care of the children and who would not hurt me. And might it even go some way to restoring my family's honor? I doubted it. It might even make things worse—a third husband at a little more than thirty years old.

But there was little time to think things through. Khanoum was dying, and I wanted to see her in Iran and still be able to return to my new life in Sweden afterward. So I said yes, hoping that he wouldn't hear the fear in my voice.

The Iranian embassy was a thirty-minute bus ride away from downtown Stockholm. It looked more like an army barracks crossed with a refugee camp than a home for diplomacy and politics.

I joined the line of people outside the metal gates and rearranged my chador for the twentieth time since leaving the house that morning. I had rarely worn one since leaving Turkey, and I hated it just as much as I had when I was a girl and the teachers at school forced me to pull it tight over my forehead to make sure that no hair was showing at all.

I wasn't sure quite what I was expecting once I got through the gates. I had pictured so many different scenarios in the previous days. Would I be treated like any other woman, given the minimum attention necessary and sent home? Or would I find myself invited into a back room for further questioning by a soldier wearing the green beret of the dreaded Sepah?

I spent hours waiting on the long wooden bench, just like every other person who sat in strained silence alongside me. And when it was finally my turn to approach the booth and explain that I wanted a visa so that I could return home and visit my dying grandmother, the warm smiles and nods from the official opposite me threw me off guard.

"But, sister," he said when I had finished talking. "A visa will take too long. Better by far to travel home on an Iranian passport. That I can get for you very quickly."

How much longer does Khanoum have? Enough time to wait for me to get a visa? If I travel under another name, as we'd already planned, perhaps it doesn't matter what passport I use. And since I'm married now to Siavash, who is a Swedish citizen, he'll likely be able to get me back into the country if I run into any problems coming back.

I filled out the paperwork, using fake family details I had memorized.

"Thank you," he said, smiling as I slid the papers back beneath the perspex window. "All you must do now is return your Swedish passport. You have no need of that anymore."

Giving up my passport worried me, but I simply nodded my thanks, said that I would do as he suggested, and left.

In less than a month I would be back at Khanoum's side. I hoped I would not be too late.

PART FOUR

IRAN AND SWEDEN

WITH EVERY SECOND THAT PASSED, the customs officer's silence grew more and more menacing. I shushed Roksana as she fidgeted beside me. I tried to compose myself. *Breathe. Stay calm. Relax.*

He was turning the pages of my Iranian passport. Every one of them was blank, but he studied them like a detective. When he finally looked up at me, his expression was blank. "Are you a refugee?"

"No."

As he held another silence, his eyes remained locked on mine. "Yes, you are. It says so right here."

He pointed to a blank box on the photo page. "If you weren't a refugee this part would be filled in. Stand aside."

I tried to protest, but two soldiers appeared and told me to follow them. I'd left Daniel in Sweden for his safety, but Roksana held on tight to me as we walked over to a door at the side of the hall.

"Not her," one of the guards said as Roksana followed me through. "She stays here."

"No! She's my daughter. She's got to stay with me. She's only a child."

"She's not coming through. She can wait here."

I searched the hall. There were some porters standing around, and I picked the nearest one and asked him to wait with her while I was inside. I pulled out $100 from my bag and bundled it into his hand. "Get her any food she wants, okay?"

His eyes bulged at the sight of the money.

Roksana's eyes were wide with fear.

"Just wait here," I told her as I tried to gently peel her away. "It'll be fine. I promise."

I was shown into a windowless room with benches along the walls and a guard at the door. Another woman my age was already in there, and she looked up, startled, when I arrived. Soon she went back to crying loudly.

I thought back to the embassy in Stockholm and the man who had smiled so nicely as he advised me to get a passport. I wanted to feel angry at him, but instead I just felt scared.

The only thing that helped was remembering the Bible. The last time I had been to the apartment near Copenhagen I had taken it with me, and I had kept it by my bed ever since. I pictured it, recalling the smell of the leather, the feathery touch of the pages. I must have held it and kissed it a hundred times already, and as I waited in the room while the woman beside me wept, I prayed for help. I didn't know if it was going to work, but I had nothing else to rely on.

I waited an hour before the door opened again. I asked the guard to take me to Roksana, but he refused. He shouted at the woman to stop crying and told me to get up and follow him.

The room I followed him into was so small, just big enough for a desk and a few chairs. In it was a man who looked as though he had lived his whole life in a cloud of cigarette smoke. He didn't try to hide the disgust in his voice as he spoke to me.

"Why did you leave Iran?"

I had rehearsed some of this already and decided to base as much as I could of my story on the truth. "It wasn't my choice. My husband told me to go with him."

He blew out a fresh cloud of smoke, made some notes, and looked back at the ID papers I had handed over along with my passport.

"And your husband, Siavash Parsan. Why did he want to leave?"

"I don't know. He didn't tell me. He just said we had to go."

The questions carried on for another while. Pretty soon they had gone full circle and I was back to explaining why I had originally left. After an hour, the man had me taken back to the waiting room. The woman was still crying.

I begged the guard at the door to let me see Roksana. He refused. "What about my family? They're waiting for me outside, and they're going to be worried. At least let me go and tell them I'm here."

I was escorted out to the arrivals hall, an armed soldier on either side of me. My two brothers, Hussein and Ali, couldn't hide their shock. The soldiers let us embrace and say a few words before taking me back.

When I finally saw the chain-smoking man from before again, he strolled into the waiting room, twirling my passport in his hands.

"We're going to need some more information."

"What do you mean?"

"I'm not happy with your explanation of why you left in the first place."

"Why? I already told you everything. Why can't you let me go?"

"Oh, you can go," he said, a hint of anger snaking its way into his voice. "You just can't ever leave."

I didn't understand. He smirked and pointed to a stamp that had appeared in my passport. "If you try and leave you'll be arrested on the spot."

His smile dropped as he stared at me. He shot his hand out. I wasn't expecting it and was too slow to avoid the slap as his palm connected with my cheek.

"Go, then. You're not worthy of calling yourself an Iranian."

———

I couldn't tell my family anything. When Hussein asked why it had taken me six hours to get out of the airport, I just shrugged and said something about there being a problem with my new passport but that it was all resolved now. Mostly, I held Roksana and tried to comfort her. She had slept a little while I was being questioned, and the old man had brought her food and drink. But she had been terrified the whole time.

It was late by the time we got to the hotel in Tehran that night and early when we left the next morning to make the hourlong flight south to Isfahan. I didn't have much time to think about what was going to happen to me, although in the few quiet moments I told myself that if I needed to, I could always get out across the mountains. *Roksana and I have done it before. We can do it again.*

There must have been over one hundred people there to greet us as we walked out at Isfahan airport. Bright red flowers were thrust into my arms; smiles, kisses, and shouts of delight rang out. In spite of all the worry that I was carrying inside, the joy of the moment was undeniable.

Eleven years had passed since I left, and in that time some people had changed beyond all recognition. Children had become parents, parents grandparents, and my little sister, Mina—born at just the same time as Roksana—had grown to be a beautiful young girl.

"Are you happy you're back in Iran?" one of my cousins asked me.

The honest answer was that I was desperate to get back to Sweden as soon as I could. "Yes," I said, knowing that the truth would only hurt their feelings and lead to questions I did not want to answer. "I am very happy."

After greeting everyone, we made our way to my parents' home. Khanoum was barely recognizable when I saw her in the courtyard. She was thin, her skin like old cloth stretched over her bones. In addition to the heart attacks, she had suffered at least one stroke. Her left side hung limp, her mouth frozen in a twisted grimace.

I held her hand and lay my head on her lap. When she tried to speak, I could not understand her words, and my sister, Mariam, came to translate.

"She said she's happy you're here," she explained. "She wants you to take her home."

The few days I spent with Khanoum back in her house on Farshadi Street were among the most precious I can remember. I sat with her in the courtyard like we once had so many years ago. The fish had long gone from the pool, and the pomegranate trees were not half as big as I remembered, but her home was an oasis. The clocks turned back to a time in my life that I had almost forgotten.

I quickly learned to understand Khanoum better, to know

when she was cold, tired, or hungry. I cooked for her, gave her baths, and changed her clothes. Again and again she told me that she was happy.

—

Life in Iran was different. It was not the same country that I had left behind. New wealth was on display, as multistory hotels rose up from the streets and factories and corporate headquarters spread out along the freeways.

There was new poverty too. When we ate out at a restaurant, children would beg outside. I had seen the same thing in Istanbul, but never before in Iran. Behind closed doors people spoke of the regime with disgust and the Sepah with fear.

A week after I arrived, I told my dad that I had to go downtown to get my passport stamped. Once the clerk had taken mine away, Dad and I sat in the crowded room together and waited. We talked a little about Khanoum's health and Daniel's progress at school. We talked about how Roksana and Mina were both growing up so fast and so well. I had already told him about divorcing Asghar and meeting Siavash but not about the fact that Siavash and I were now married. I thought about it but chose not to. I wanted to carry on sitting, father and daughter, just talking about the everyday things in life. Most of all, I wanted to remember what it felt like to have him fight for me, to take my side and defend me even when I was fully to blame. Until then, I hadn't realized quite how deeply I missed being the one he fought for.

It didn't take me long to remember the Iranian concept of time, especially when sitting in a building staffed by officials. But as those waiting for their passports were called up, given their papers, and dismissed, and the crowd disappeared, I worried.

We were the last two in the room when a woman came over to us and told us that since it was noon and they were about to close we had to leave.

"But what about my passport? I need to get it stamped."

"Oh," she said. "You're Parsan?"

I nodded.

"We had to send that one to the other office. You're going to have to get it from them."

As soon as we were back on the street Dad pointed at the scrap of paper the lady had given me with the address I needed to visit. "That's not a good place," he said. "I've heard of it. The Sepah works out of there."

That was my nightmare, right there. Me being questioned by the regime's brutal military police. Me walking into a Sepah jail and never walking out. Me hanging by the neck from a crane in a public market.

"I'm worried about you," Dad said. "I'm really worried."

———

The camera overlooking the street was clearly visible. "Don't come with me, Dad," I said as we stood on the corner and watched the entrance. Two armed guards stood out front, their green berets and uniforms confirming what Dad had said. "I don't want to get you into trouble."

"No," he said, squeezing my hand. "I'm coming with you."

I tried to remember what it meant to act like a good Muslim woman as I crossed the street. I dropped my eyes and fell in behind Dad, grateful for his escort. Muslim women were always safe when they were with their fathers, weren't they?

"Not him," the guard said after I explained why I was there. "Only you."

I turned around and embraced Dad. "Go home," I whispered. "Tell Hussein and Ali where I am, and see if they know anyone who can help."

Dad looked at me, nodded, and left.

I tried to be brave and turned back to the building. After taking a deep breath, I walked inside.

The corridor was just like the one in the Hotel back in Turkey. Long, straight, dark, with closed, windowless doors on either side every few paces. I was not handcuffed, but I was in no doubt that I was their prisoner.

I was put in a room, told to sit down and wait. The door locked behind me.

I noticed the table was fixed to the floor. The chairs too. Barred windows were blacked out. Even the air tasted stale and trapped.

The Sepah guard who came in didn't introduce himself or try to get me on his side. He just sat opposite me and went straight at it.

"Where have you been living?"

"I've come from Sweden."

"How did you get there?"

"We flew. My husband arranged it all."

"Really?"

"Yes."

"And why did he need to get out?"

"I don't know. He never told me. He just said we were leaving, and so I left with him."

"For Sweden."

"Yes."

"By plane."

"Yes."

"So you had a passport? And a visa?"

"Yes. He arranged it all."

"But this passport you came in with, it wasn't the same one?"

"No, I lost the last one."

"You lost it."

"Yes."

It went on like that for an hour, maybe more. I knew my story was weak, and I knew that he knew it too. The more questions he asked, the further away from me the answers slipped.

"I'm sorry," I said at one point. "I'm very tired."

He stood up, chewing his lip as he stared at me.

"Yes," he said. "You're tired, and we need to go and do some investigating into this story of yours. You can leave for now, but report back here at 8 a.m. tomorrow. You understand?"

I tried to brush aside everyone's concerns when I got home, but it was impossible. I might have been out of the country for a long time, but even I knew the reputation that the Sepah had for brutality, especially against women. When I told them I had to go back the next day, my mother let out a cry.

The same guard questioned me again on the second day. And on the third, the fourth, the fifth, and so on. Every morning I presented myself at the gate at 8 a.m. and was taken inside and down the corridor. About the only thing that changed was the interrogation room, but since they were all identical anyway, it made no difference at all.

I would sit, sometimes alone, sometimes facing the guard, for hours. Every day at 4 p.m. I was released, always with the same instruction to return the next morning.

I knew that I couldn't let the guard know anything about Asghar. Siavash had left illegally, like almost every other refugee from Iran, but he hadn't fled the regime. He had simply gotten himself smuggled across the border into Turkey because he was hoping for a better life. I was confident that the regime had nothing on file about him, and as long as the guard believed that it was with Siavash that I left, the damage would be limited.

If he found out the truth, however, I knew that things would be different. There would be no more passes home at the end of the day, that was for sure. Not only had Asghar been labeled a plotter against the regime, but his activities in Denmark and Sweden in support of the Shah were bound to have been noticed. If the guard knew I was Asghar's wife, I'd either be dead in a matter of weeks or jailed for the rest of my life.

If I had ever had any questions about whether it was right to marry Siavash, those doubts completely vanished in Iran. Without Siavash's name on my ID card, I would never have been allowed to return home at the end of each day's questioning.

The strain of keeping up the lie was starting to show. I couldn't sleep, couldn't eat, and I couldn't even relax when I was at home; for the sake of everyone I loved, I had to keep the truth from them as well.

After weeks of being questioned, something changed in the guard's tone. He started sounding more menacing, dropping hints that after he was done with me I'd be sent somewhere far worse. He talked about how he wanted to keep me safe, how there were other people, powerful people, who had taken an interest in my case. If I didn't help him, they would send someone else to do the job. "And you won't like the way they treat you at all."

All along, whenever I wasn't frantically reminding myself of the script I had decided to stick to, I was picturing myself crouched on the floor by the side of my bed, the Bible in my hands, prayers flowing from my lips. I tried to remember the nuns in the convent and the way I felt as I sat on the chair outside their meeting room. "Help me," I prayed silently. "Jesus, help me."

When the guard finally snapped, slamming his fist on the table and shouting at the top of his voice, the guard reminded me so much of Asghar. His eyes locked on mine, and the veins in his throat throbbed. "We know you're lying! We have no record whatsoever of any passport ever being issued to you and no visa either. We know you escaped illegally, and you'll go to jail for that."

—

After the Sepah finally finished with me, I was told to report in a couple of weeks to a court near the airport. The location was different, but the routine the same, and for a few more days after my first visit I made the journey there every morning. I sat all day, waiting in yet another small, locked room, as the mullahs discussed my case away from me.

In the end, their verdict was that my case was special and that I needed to visit a court in Tehran. "You did a bad thing by fleeing the country illegally," the mullah told me as I stood, eyes down, before him. "The police will escort you."

At that, I was taken away. Handcuffs bit into my skin as I

was pushed into a car and driven to the airport. I begged the officer sitting beside me to remove them, but he ignored me. Only when we walked through the departures hall together, attracting stares from everyone I passed, did he finally agree to undo them. It cost me $500, but it was worth every cent.

In Tehran, I was told that I would have to wait for my case to be heard. I sat through a series of interviews with other guards and police officers. Each one asked the same questions about how and why I left and what I knew about Siavash.

Eventually, they moved me on from the interviews, and I stood before the judge. He was a mullah dressed in the traditional black robes of an Islamic cleric. There was a Sepah guard beside me, a court secretary to one side, and a long bench behind me where five men in handcuffs and prison uniforms sat.

I was terrified. I was at the end of all the courage and hope that had kept me going throughout weeks of questioning and waiting on my own in locked rooms. I was sleep-deprived, underfed, and worn out from reminding myself what to tell and what to withhold. I had barely seen Roksana since we arrived in Iran, and Khanoum was getting worse.

I was crying so much that my coat was wet with tears. They were laughing. Everyone in the room was laughing at me.

The mullah repeated his question. "Tell me one more time, why are you crying?"

My plan to fly back and spend a week in the country I had risked my life to flee and then simply fly home again afterward seemed so foolish now. What was I thinking? Had I really believed that I could come and go as if Iran were like Italy or Ireland?

The mullah had started off asking me about my life, about why I had left, and what I was doing in Sweden. He mocked me for fumbling my words and led the others in a chorus of laughter when I told him I was worried about my daughter, that Iran was no longer my home, and that I just wanted to go back to Sweden.

"Oh, so you want to go back to Sweden now, do you?"

More laughter.

"And what is it that you so despise about our humble country? Are the men too dark for you? You prefer the fair-skinned man, do you?"

He was playing to the crowd and loving it.

That was when I started to cry.

Their laughter increased. I didn't care. Inside I was starting to do the one thing that I could. I said silent prayers, screaming them so loud that they filled my head. I remembered the lesson Khanoum taught me once, about how important it was to say, "Mohammed, help me" one hundred times.

Jesus, help me.

Jesus, help me.

Jesus, help me.

Over and over I pleaded.

This was my last chance.

The mullah calmed the crowd, wiped his eyes, and laid out the facts for me. "For leaving the country without authorization—six months in jail. For falsely obtaining a passport—six months in jail. So that's one year in jail and a $1,000 fine."

His words winded me. I felt Roksana and Daniel disappear. I thought about the bond I once feared had been severed between Daniel and me—the one that had grown back since we left Asghar. If I went to jail as the mullah said, I feared the bond would be cut all over again, and not just with Daniel, but Roksana too.

I promise you, Jesus, if you help me I will follow you. I will do what the nuns do. I will give my life to serving you.

The court was silent for a while.

"Okay," said the mullah, folding his hands across his chest. "How about I take off the jail time. You pay $1,000, you happy then?"

I stared up at him, surprised but nodding frantically. "Yes, of course."

"Come here," he said softly. "Be careful. Don't cry. And when you get back to Sweden, you get me a visa, okay? I would very much like to visit you."

I swallowed whatever confusion and repulsion I felt and tried to smile. "Of course I will."

Dad and Hussein were both waiting outside the court. They looked shocked when they saw me walking toward them, but there was not time to explain.

"I can't speak," I told them, looking for a taxi. "Let's go first."

I handed over my paperwork and paid the $1000 fine at the bank, and then we went to the police station to pick up my passport.

The clerk looked surprised when he came back from checking for it. "It's not here. We sent it back to Isfahan."

"Why?" I asked.

"We didn't think you'd be needing it."

I had been in Iran for almost three months. With two days left until my ticket home expired, I stood at the bus stop in

Isfahan surrounded by my family. Roksana chatted happily in Farsi to her aunts, uncles, cousins, and grandparents. I remembered how, when we arrived, she could barely string a sentence together. Somehow, while I had been held, questioned, and pushed around the country, she had become fluent. She had grown up as well.

I cried as I hugged so many people. There was sorrow within me, knowing that I might never return again. But mostly there were tears of relief.

Khanoum stood to embrace me. "Are you happy?" she asked as I held her tight. I couldn't tell her any of the story that I wanted to, but I could tell her this much.

"Yes," I said. "I think I am."

As the bus engine started I watched Khanoum peel away from the crowd and come stand on the side on which we were sitting. Both she and I were crying. She had kept her promise. She had waited for me.

When we pulled out, she took a few steps forward, one arm raised to wave us off. I watched her trip and fall. Several people ran to help. Soon she was lost within the crowd. Sadly, within less than a week she would pass on.

———

It took three days before we could do it, but as soon as it was possible, I took Daniel and Roksana with me to a church in Stockholm.

It was open but empty. None of us spoke as we lit candles at the back, or as we walked down toward the front and sat on a pew. Though the church was dark, the lights that shone within it were bright, bright enough to outshine all the darkness and fear and pain that I had known over the years.

I felt free. I felt known. I felt happy in a way I had not experienced for far, far too long.

I thought about all the pain and heartache I'd survived. I thought about the people along the way who'd been a ray of kindness in the middle of all the darkness: the officer's wife in Turkey who had taken care of me and Roksana; the Roma woman at the refugee center who had offered me food and money to call home; the English-speaking strangers who had brought me the Bible in Farsi; Sadaf; Reza; Anna—all people God had used to watch over me as I searched for peace and safety.

I thought back to the time in the convent. I thought about Sister Elisabeth and her joy-filled smile. I remembered looking through the half-open door, the sound of praying filling my ears.

I shifted in my pew and knelt down. My eyes closed, I could feel Daniel and Roksana kneeling on either side of me. Even they didn't know everything that had happened in Iran, and I had kept what I could of Asghar's violence away from them, but Jesus knew. He knew everything.

When I spoke, my voice filled the church.

"We are Christians now. From now on, we are yours."

THE JOY REMAINED, BUT PRETTY SOON

I had some practical problems to face. I had no money and no job, and I had an uncomfortable feeling that I had not heard the last from the regime or even the mullah in Tehran who had asked me to help him visit.

So, with childlike faith, I prayed and waited expectantly for answers.

They came quickly.

Straight after leaving the church I started my search for employment, praying as I went. Within twenty-four hours I landed a job as a dressmaker. My boss was a Christian and the most generous and kind man I had ever met. Prayer, God reminded me, works.

I prayed for a new home too. It took a little longer to see the answer to that one come to pass, but sure enough, within a few months, I was standing inside a beautiful old house that we really should not have been able to afford, giving thanks yet again for the ways in which God had provided.

I began a new routine. After working in the day I would visit the house to carry on the job of stripping walls, sanding wood, and giving the rooms the first lick of paint they had seen in years. It took three months in all, but by the end of it we were able to move in. Daniel and Roksana finally had their own bed-rooms, and there was even one for Sara, Siavash's daughter who had joined us from Iran.

Soon, my boss approached me with an offer of help that opened up new opportunities I had never dreamed would be mine. He told me that he thought I was a hard worker, that he wanted to help, and that, if ever I wanted to start my own busi-ness, he would let me take whatever material and tools I needed from his shop and pay him back when I could.

My routine changed a little. Instead of picking up a paintbrush after work, I came home and carried on sewing. I made the kind of clothes that I saw on the well-dressed women of Stockholm, elegant dresses and classic pants. There was not a chador in sight.

All this hard work meant that I had little time for other things. I went to church most Sundays, sitting at the back near the candles, letting the sounds wash over me. The air always felt richer in there, and I would leave at the end of the service grateful for the moments of still and calm in the middle of a busy week.

Going to church was about as public as my faith got. I didn't talk about my Christian beliefs with anyone, just as I didn't talk at all about the rest of my life before returning to Sweden. Faith was private. I liked it that way.

What I didn't anticipate was to hear a knock on my door one Saturday morning and to find our elderly Iranian neighbors asking my family to join them for prayer later that evening.

Ever since leaving Denmark I had tried to live far away from Iranian communities, and when we moved in to our tumbledown house I had no idea that the families around were anything other than good old-fashioned Swedes.

I realized I was wrong soon after we moved. The house five doors down from ours was even bigger and more ramshackle than ours, and it was home to an old couple with gray hair, olive skin, and thick Iranian accents.

At least she didn't wear a chador. I had consoled myself every time we exchanged nods and smiles out on the sidewalk.

But being asked to join them for prayer? That was an unexpected and unpleasant surprise. I had no intention of getting involved with any Muslims whatsoever, and I could feel the fear begin to inch up my throat.

"I'm sorry," I said. "Tonight we're busy."

They smiled and left, and that was that. The rest of the day was given over to the usual mix of household chores and errands, and by the time the afternoon drew to a close I had put the invitation out of my mind.

I answered the door later to the husband when he knocked early that evening.

"Hello!" he said brightly, waving an envelope. "I wonder if you could help me? I have this letter from the government that I don't understand. Could you translate it for me?"

When I was done helping, he looked me right in the eyes. "We're waiting for you to join us, you know. Come on!"

This guy didn't let up. I was done being polite and Swedish about it. I needed to change my defense. "Listen, mister, don't talk to me about God. I'm not a Muslim, and I'm not interested in praying with you."

His smile didn't waver. "Please, just come. Bring your family too. My wife and I would love to meet them."

Maybe the only way of getting rid of him was to play along. I swallowed hard and said that we'd be down in a few minutes.

———

The sight of almost twenty pairs of shoes lined up on the porch outside the house made me want to turn tail and run. But it was the sound of the singing that came from within the house that compelled me to go inside.

The melody was simple, almost like a ballad from my youth. It was the sound of warmth, of love.

Inside the room was packed. People stood elbow to elbow, and the singing pressed deep within me. Some were crying, some praying with eyes closed. Of the rest, all eyes were on the words projected on the wall at the front. I only had to read a few lines before the sobbing started.

When I come to you with a broken heart, you're there for me
When I come to you with a broken heart, you answer me
When I cry for your cross, you hear and heal me still

I had never seen or heard the words before—I had never heard Christians sing anything but the liturgy during a church service—but it was as if they had been written just for me. They were the prayer I had never been able to speak for myself, but which said everything I ever wanted to say.

My knees gave way, and I sank to the floor. I could feel every moment of pain I had ever endured welling up within me and forcing its way out through my sobs. I could not stop. At times I

could barely breathe, but I knew that whatever was happening.
God was in control.

The singing had softened to a murmur by the time I could
open my eyes and talk. The old man was in front of me, smiling.

"I'm a Christian too," I said.

"Really?" he said. "We didn't know. We thought you were a
Muslim."

It was my turn to smile then.

"So are you baptized?"

I frowned. "What's 'baptized'?"

———

Back home that night, I sat next to Siavash and watched the video
tape we had been sent home with. It told the story of Jesus's life,
death, and resurrection. By the time the two hours were up, my heart
was changed. I finally saw what it fully meant to be a Christian, to
want to live life in pursuit of Him. I prayed the prayer that filled the
film's final few minutes and asked Him to come into my life.

I was so happy to knock on my neighbors' door the next
morning. "I want to be baptized," I told them. "I've been praying
all night, and I know what it means to truly give my life to Jesus.
Can you baptize me now?"

"Now? No, it's too soon. You need to learn about Jesus first.
That takes time."

"But I've been learning about him for years. I really want to
get baptized."

He thought awhile. "We don't have a priest or a pastor, but
there's one we know. Maybe he can help you work out what to do."

I couldn't wait a moment longer, so as soon as I had the address of the church nearby, I took the bus into town.

The church was like no other church I had been in before. From the outside it looked more like an office than a place of worship. Inside there were no candles at the back and no hollow echo of my footsteps as I walked down the front. There was just an old carpet in a room that looked as though it had been used for many different purposes.

I found the pastor, another Iranian man. I told him that my neighbor had suggested I visit so that he could baptize me.

"Okay," he said as we sat on plastic chairs at the front of the room. "How long ago did you come to Jesus?"

"Yesterday."

He looked confused, so I carried on talking. I told him about the Farsi Bible and the nuns and how I had prayed in the court in Tehran and how God had answered my prayers then and so many other times as well.

He was smiling when I finally stopped.

"Okay. We'll do it whenever you're ready."

I picked a date twenty days ahead and decided that if I was going to get baptized, I wanted some witnesses who would be surprised. So I phoned my sister Mariam in Isfahan.

"Do you want to come to Sweden?"

"Sure. When?"

"I'm thinking soon. Like three weeks."

"Three weeks? You know a visa takes six months, don't you?"

I did. I also knew that God is not subject to the same rules as government officials. I told Mariam and then Hussein that they should apply the next day and expect to be with me by the end of the month. I could hear the doubt in both their voices.

Two weeks passed before Mariam called, amazed to be holding her visa in her hand. Hussein had not been so fortunate, but I told him to pack a bag and drive Mariam to Tehran anyway. And I suggested that they bring Mariam's son, Davood, too.

Getting the visa was easy, but finding the plane tickets was tough. I phoned a tour operator and asked whether she had two tickets leaving in four days' time. She didn't.

An hour later the phone rang. Of course, it was the tour operator. "I've just had someone cancel. I have four tickets available exactly when you want them."

Hussein's visa was issued by the time he reached Tehran, and Mariam's son was able to pick his up at the Swedish embassy on the way to the airport.

As amazing as all this was, I trusted that God had even more in store for them when they arrived.

———

Almost every Iranian knows two things about Armenia, the country that meets Iran at its northern border. They know that it is full of Christians and that it is an excellent place to take a vacation from all the stress that goes with living under Islamic rule.

This is why Hussein looked so confused when we sat down in my house and I told him that I was going to be baptized as a Christian the very next day.

"You mean that you are to become an Armenian?"

"No, Hussein. I'm a Christian."

He thought awhile. "Okay, I respect your choice, but why?"

I didn't need to think at all. Since that night when I visited my neighbor's house, the answer was never far from my lips. "Because Jesus did everything for me."

He looked stunned.

Mariam, on the other hand, looked skeptical. "This doesn't sound so good. Maybe for you it is, but not for us."

My baptism service didn't leave them convinced, but it didn't send Mariam or Hussein away either. Throughout the whole two months that they stayed in Sweden, every time I suggested they come with me to church they both said yes. Even when it meant joining three thousand other people to hear a well-known pastor from Hollywood who believed that God's power is just as strong today as it ever was.

The place was packed, and we had no choice but to stand at the side. That meant we had a good view of everything that happened when the preacher invited people to stand and started to pray.

When the first person fell over, we all stared.

The second one fell soon after. None of us had ever seen anything like it, but I knew that whatever was going on was something that smelt of God.

Hussein, not so much.

"Ha!" he said, a little too loudly as more and more people slumped backward, some into their seats, some all the way down onto the floor. "Look at them all! That guy on stage must have bribed them to do it."

I didn't have time to stay and explain to my brother what was going on. I just knew that I had to get down to the front and be prayed for myself.

The preacher was looking my way as I picked my way through the crowd. "Lord," he prayed, "send your fire."

My legs went the moment he said "fire." I was down, but I felt as though I was being lifted up by God's love. It came in waves, again and again, speaking to every cell within me of the depth of God's love for me.

I felt a hand on my shoulder, shaking me. I opened my eyes to see Mariam and Hussein above me.

"What happened?" said Hussein. "Are you okay? Did they give you money too?"

I sat up and reassured him that I was fine and hadn't been paid a thing. The preacher was nearby, so I waved him over. Soon he was praying for my brother and sister. It didn't take long for Hussein to fall to the floor, shaking and crying out, "God, forgive me! Forgive me for what I've said!"

Mariam and Hussein both returned home to Iran having asked Jesus to save them and pledging to follow him for the rest of their lives. As soon as Hussein told his wife and Mariam told her husband, they discovered how much that choice would cost them. Both marriages soon ended in divorce.

"It is not easy here," said Mariam on the phone. "We can't worship in public, and there is a lot of anger toward us. We have to keep our faith secret."

My heart went out to my sister and my brother. It was no easy thing to be a Christian in Iran. They hadn't even been able to tell our mom and dad the truth before our parents had moved away.

My parents, aware of the growing disdain with which people in Isfahan were treating the family, knew that it was time for them to leave. They'd gone through the work of applying for and obtaining visas, packed up my younger sister, Mina, and moved to Sweden to be with me.

Soon after they arrived I was serving the family a meal while I listened to my dad tell stories of how bad things had gotten.

"People talk," he said. "And now Mina has no future there. We can never go back."

He spoke about the way people now viewed our family, about the problems each and every one of them had faced as our list of transgressions had grown longer and longer. "Even Hussein and Mariam are divorced now."

I wondered if he was blaming me. But his voice carried no anger, and it held no spite. It was, instead, just tired. He listed the troubles the way an old man lists his ailments, holding out for as long as he could, but full of the knowledge that in time they would win.

I felt guilty. I had always felt guilty. From the moment they first pleaded with me to divorce Asghar and I had choked back the tears to tell them I could not, I had locked my secrets away from them. I hated it, but what could I do? Lying to them—about why I stayed with Asghar, about why we left Iran, about why I'd had to leave Daniel behind, about why we did not speak to them for five months, about why the Sepah wanted to talk to me—all of it had been my only way of keeping them safe.

But I was done lying. It was time for the truth.

"Mom, Dad, I have something I need to tell you. I am a Christian."

Mom's anger was immediate. "What? How could you? We're not even finished dealing with your divorce, and now you say you're a Christian. Have you heard nothing that your father has just said? Your sisters, your brothers, even your cousins, they're all affected by what you've done. How do you expect them to live with this? It's not right."

"I love my God. I love Jesus. I'm never going back to Islam."

Mom stared at me. Dad, his arms folded, stared at the food. Mina had gone off to play with Roksana and Daniel. Siavash and his daughter had gone out. Nobody was eating.

"Do you remember when I was in the court and the mullah suddenly let me go? That wasn't just luck, and it wasn't just chance. It was prayer. I prayed to Jesus to help me, and he did. Or do you remember when I got back and needed a job? I prayed, and that very same day I got one. Don't you see? It's all real."

Mom waved a hand. Dad carried on staring. None of what I was saying was taking root. So I tried something else.

"I had a friend who worked for me at the boutique. She couldn't get pregnant. For ten years she went to the mosque and did just as the mullahs told her to but still nothing. I was telling her about Jesus answering prayer and said we could pray. Her husband was a communist and he didn't believe in God at all, but they both came here and I told them again that if Jesus can rise from the dead he can help couples get pregnant. So I put my hand on her stomach and prayed. The next month she was pregnant.

"When she was six months pregnant she came into work and told me that her husband didn't want her to have any more contact with me, so she quit. Three months later her husband called. He said that she was at the hospital, and the doctors couldn't find the baby's heartbeat. He wanted me to come and pray. So I went.

The baby was dead, and the doctors were telling her that she needed to go home and wait for labor to start so her body could expel the baby's body. They said it might take almost a week. Can you imagine having to wait that long? So I prayed again. Five minutes later the baby was born. Even in the sadness of losing their child, the husband knew that God had helped. And my friend said that she knew that God would help them conceive again. Just last week she told me that she's pregnant again."

Mom was not listening. Nor was Dad. I so wanted to be able to convince them of the truth of what had happened and the power of God, but as I heard myself tell the story, I could feel their unbelief.

We all just pushed the food around our plates that night. It was not the kind of reunion I had hoped for.

When it was time to go to bed I grabbed Mom by the hand. "What do you want Jesus to do for you? What's the one thing that would help you trust him?"

"If he comes to me in my dreams tonight, then I will believe in him."

She knew I had no power to make that happen. "Okay," I said, "I'm going to pray that he does just that."

Dad went to bed soon after as well, and as I cleared the table I told God that I was weak and powerless to help. If he really was going to break through to my mom, he had to do it himself.

"I believe you can do it, God," I prayed out loud.

———

I was expectant the next morning. I knew that Mom had met Jesus in the night—not because of anything I'd heard, but simply because I trusted God completely.

She was silent from the moment she entered the kitchen. I asked how she was, gently probing for signs. I got none. Only silence.

Things stayed that way for most of the day. When she did talk, it was through gritted teeth. I began to doubt my earlier certainty.

At breakfast the following morning, I decided to take a different approach. I said nothing. Mom was soon crying.

"What happened?" I asked. "What did I do?"

"That night you prayed, I did have a dream. A man came, and he was holding a shovel. He dug up some earth and put a seed in the hole. Then he turned to me and said, 'You can do it.' He reached out to give me some seed, and when I looked I saw that he had a hole in his hand. He wasn't like any other man I'd seen. He was light."

Mom had never heard anything about Jesus, apart from a line or two in the Qur'an about him being a prophet. She knew nothing about the holes in his hands or the way the Bible describes him as the light of the world. But none of that mattered. She had met Jesus for herself that first night in Sweden. From then on nothing would ever be the same.

I was so grateful to God and so relieved as well. I never doubted that he could reveal himself to my mom, but I wondered whether she would have eyes to see. To know that he had heard and answered my prayer was a wonderful thing.

Even more wonderful was the fact that two months later my mom, my dad, and my sister Mina were all baptized.

I HAD PRAYED HARD ABOUT MY PARENTS coming to Sweden. Part of me had been scared of them coming to live with me and potentially being unhappy when they found out about my faith in Christ. If that was going to happen, I would rather they stayed in Iran. But when they got their visas within a month, and then both Mom and Dad, as well as Mina, became Christians so soon after their arrival, I was sure that all my fears had been in vain.

And, for a time, I was right. Life was good. Being reunited with my parents and seeing both them and my little sister take their first steps of faith was a privilege and a joy. We went to church as a family and studied the Bible together, along with those gray-haired neighbors down the road. To be able to live free alongside them under the same roof brought healing to some deep, old wounds.

But life under that one roof also started to get crowded. Mom, Dad, and Mina squeezed in along with Siavash and me, Roksana, Daniel, and Siavash's daughter Sara. Soon, Siavash's mom and brother arrived from Iran and moved in as well. The house had felt big when it was just the five of us living there. With ten of us in it, there was barely any room to breathe.

The cramped conditions added extra stress to Siavash's and my marriage. While I had been passionately pursuing my newfound faith, Siavash had stalled. He hadn't gone back to Islam, but he hadn't trusted his life to Jesus either.

Then, after six years of marriage, Siavash moved out.

It was a bad time. In the sadness and tears there were echoes of so many other bad times in my life. Feelings of loss, sorrow, and worry all took up residence within me. But the darker the skies, the more I knew that only God could help me though.

Yet even though I was desperate for him to help me, a part of me was still holding back. At church my pastor repeatedly told me that I, too, was going to be a pastor one day, that I would travel the world and preach. *No way*, I thought. Why would I want to? I had my business and my life, and both of them demanded more of me than I felt like I had to offer.

I was sitting alone in my bedroom one day, looking at a flower I had been keeping alive for months. Overnight, quite without warning, it had died. A small pile of curling petals lay at its base.

I couldn't have found a better picture of my life at that time. In the space of just a few months, it was as if a bomb had gone off within it.

By this time, the kids were grown. Daniel had moved out, and so had Roksana. She had headed up north of Stockholm to enroll at a Bible college. I loved her passion and commitment to her faith, but between the monthly fees I couldn't afford to pay and the fears for both of their safety that visited me every night as I tried to sleep, the stress was starting to build.

Mina was unwell in the hospital and didn't seem to be getting better.

My parents were approaching the end of their allowed stay in the country, and all their appeals for leave to remain had been rejected.

Siavash had filed for a divorce. He was playing tough, asking for half the house and half my business—a business which had been thriving for so long but was now on the brink of collapse.

I could not keep up with my car payments. I owed $50,000 in tax payments that I had missed in order to pay my workers' wages. According to my accountant, I was about to find myself in real trouble. At times I couldn't even afford the train fare to get into work.

I was unhappy and depressed. I cried uncontrollably. Every day.

There was not a single leaf that had not fallen from the flower.

———

"Annahita," my pastor said again after church one day. "You'll be a great pastor. All this? It's just the testing."

I didn't have the energy to tell him that being a pastor was the last thing on my mind. But his words didn't go unnoticed. I thought about the testing as I walked home that day. I remembered what had happened to Job in the Bible, and how, even in the midst of tragedy, he had stayed firm in his faith in God.

By the time I reached the house, I was praying out loud.

"If you think I'm going back to Islam, you're wrong. I'm not going back. I'm like Job. So many bad things have happened in my life, but I trust my God. I always will."

———

I ended up having to sell everything to pay my taxes. Even my bed. But then, little by little, things started to improve. Mina got better and came home. My parents were told they could stay.

Roksana transferred home, and the business started to grow again. After a year the house had furniture again. After two, the business had expanded enough for me to buy a new boutique on the other side of the city.

I took out a loan and paid Siavash every dollar he asked for and thanked God for the power to forgive him.

"Annahita," my pastor didn't give up. "You've got to go to Bible school. How else are you going to make it as a pastor?"

"Pastor," I begged him. "Can we please stop having this conversation? I'm never going to be a pastor."

———

I gave in eventually, but only to a few of my pastor's requests for help in ministry. He had asked me to serve with a group of Iranian Christians, and I met with them regularly in the church. We prayed together, studied the Bible, and talked about what it means to be a Christian. It was a sweet time, but things changed when a church leader from Iran joined the group. He didn't believe a woman should be helping to lead. He made it clear that I was not welcome.

It wasn't hard to back off. I knew all along that my pastor's encouragements toward ministry were just that—nice words intended to give me a little confidence boost. I was never going to be a pastor, and now I had the proof of why.

———

By now, my parents had their own apartment, and I phoned them one day as I was driving back from work. I told them I'd be there soon, and Mom said she'd set an extra place at the table.

Just after I hung up, I happened to glance to my right, only to see my field of vision dominated by an SUV driving straight at me.

All I had time to do was pray.

God, help me!

When my mom heard the sound of sirens, she looked out of the window. Something didn't feel right, somehow, and she called my cell. The voice that answered it belonged to a stranger. As soon as she heard them talk about a crash, she ran out of the apartment to find me.

My injuries were severe, but not life threatening. My little Peugeot had not stood up well to the Volvo, and I had been pulled out of the tailgate by the emergency crew that arrived on the scene. I'd broken three ribs and needed surgery to fix the place where the broken gearstick had pierced my hand. But it was my legs that had taken the biggest beating.

"Your kneecaps were like eggshells," the doctor told me. "They'd been forced halfway up your thigh."

After eleven days in the hospital I was allowed to go home. With both legs and one hand in plaster I was confined to the couch and unable to do much of anything for myself. God had me all to himself.

It took me four months to be able to walk unaided, but much less time to realize that I had gone away from what God wanted. I had closed my eyes and ears to him, and for that I was deeply sorry.

"God," I prayed. "I promise I'm coming back to you. I'll serve you. Just please don't make me go back to working among Muslims again. Other than that, I'm all in."

God's response was clear.

"You are lying!"

I didn't understand. I had meant every word I said; I was willing to go all in for him. But the more I prayed, the more I understood. How could I claim to be really serving him if I put my own conditions on what he was calling me to do? How could I claim to be all in if a part of me was so closed?

———

The elevators were all in use when I arrived at the hospital. I joined the knot of people waiting by the closed metal doors, their eyes locked on the display above and the numbers that counted slowly up and down. It suited me fine to wait awhile. I needed to think.

I could still feel the dream of a few nights earlier in my mind. It lingered within me like woodsmoke on a winter scarf. I let myself drift back, my imagination folded within the words I knew were from God.

There had been no images in my dream, no people or places. Only words. The dream was like a thought I did not think myself or a voice I heard deep within my bones. But it felt more real than most. Three times I heard the words from Matthew 18, "If your brother or sister sins, go and point out their fault."

As soon as I woke up I knew what it meant.

A few months before my accident, I had watched a well-dressed Muslim woman a little older than me walk into the shop one Friday afternoon. She ignored my customary greeting and looked around the dresses, flicking them along the rails with her hands while her eyes scanned the store. I knew she was not interested in buying anything. Women in head scarves rarely shopped in my boutiques.

When I finished with the other customer and the door closed behind her, the woman walked up to me. It surprised me how soft her voice was as she spoke.

"I hear that you are a Christian," she said, her eyes still scanning the room. I nodded my reply. It was no secret that I went to church, though I did not make a habit of talking about it with Muslim strangers.

When she next spoke, her eyes locked on mine. "Can you tell me about Jesus?" She said his name as though the very syllables themselves were both precious and dangerous. I knew I had nothing to fear from her. I knew I had to say yes.

For the next three months Sarina and I met most weeks in the back of my shop and talked about Jesus. We prayed and read the Bible, and the more Sarina heard about the Son of God, the more she fell in love with him.

But it had all stopped the day my phone rang.

"Annahita Parsan?" said the voice in heavy Farsi.

"Yes."

"You have been talking blasphemy to my wife!" He was shouting now, the rage hurting my ears and setting my heart racing. "You are haram, and the Qur'an allows me to kill you for what you have done. If you see her again you will die."

I was scared. For days I felt as though I was going to suffocate beneath memories of Asghar's attacks and the horrors of the Hotel. I feared what would happen if this man ever came to make good on his threat, and so I did exactly what he said. When I received no more visits from Sarina, I made no attempt to contact her myself.

The car crash had put Sarina and her husband out of my mind. But as I lay on the couch with my legs and arm locked in place, prayers of repentance and surrender formed on my lips, and my mind had started to drift to her again.

Not long after I could talk again, I had the dream. I knew it was about Sarina and her husband. I had been sinned against and threatened, and in response I had hidden when really I should have trusted God more. After all, hadn't he promised to protect me? Wasn't his love the thing that had already brought my daughter back from the dead and saved me from prison not once but twice?

The very next day after the dream I looked up in the shop to see a woman standing in front of me. "Do you know Sarina?" she asked.

"Yes."

"She is sick and in the hospital. She has cancer."

I did not know what to say.

"She is sad that you have not been in touch. Will you visit her?"

What could I do? I nodded and asked for the hospital details.

———

I stepped carefully out of the elevator and walked the short distance to the bed in the corner of the ward that Sarina's friend had described. But before my eyes could pick out my friend, they rested on a man I knew could only be her husband.

He looked up at me, his stare like the wolves from the mountain that sometimes crept into my dreams. Did he know who I was? I could not be sure. I tried a smile, but none came.

He was standing on the other side of the bed. Sarina was lying there, her eyes closed. Drips and monitors stood like silent sentries around her. She looked pale and weak, and inside I felt a thousand prayers explode as I pleaded with God to heal her.

When I looked back across the bed again his heavy-lidded eyes were still on me. This time they could not conceal the hatred within him.

"Why are you here?" he hissed in the same thick accent I remembered from the phone call. "This is all your fault. Allah has punished her for becoming a Christian. You crushed my life."

I thought about running, but I knew I wanted to stay. I wanted to get away, but I also wanted to be close to God. I wanted to trust him, and I knew that meant staying right where I was.

I thought about the words from my dream. Should I do as Scripture said and tell this man that he had sinned against me? I had no idea what to do, so I looked back at Sarina and prayed silent prayers. I pleaded for her healing but also for protection. I was desperate, powerless, and unable to do anything but pray. Only God could rescue me. Only God could rescue him.

We stayed like that for some minutes—my eyes on Sarina, her husband's eyes on me. Then she started to stir. When she looked my way she was anything but weak and pale. Her eyes were wide and full of life. Her hand reached out for mine.

"Can you see him here, Annahita? Can you see him? Jesus is here with me. He says I'll be all right. I'm coming back to life!"

Her husband was still for a moment, as if he was slowly deciphering the true meaning of Sarina's words. And then he exploded. He stepped toward Sarina, grabbed her by the shoulders, and started to shake. She gasped and tried to draw back, but he was too strong. I shouted at him to stop, and for some reason he listened. He froze, staring at his wife. Her eyes were shut tight, but still the tears leaked out.

He turned to me. "You!" he said, rounding the foot of the bed with a few short steps. He grabbed my shoulder and spun me round, pushing me out of the room so fast that I could do nothing to stop him. He bundled me toward the elevator that was already open and waiting. "When you come back I will kill you," he said as he threw me between the doors.

I watched him turn and march back toward Sarina. The doors closed in front of me. I shut my eyes, ignored the pain in my knees, and carried on praying.

———

I didn't have a strategy, and I didn't have a plan, but visiting and praying for Sarina marked a change for me. From then on I decided to follow God the only way I really knew how: to open my eyes and say yes to the invitations that he continued to lay before me. Once I decided to do that, the opportunities flooded in. Like the young Muslim man from Afghanistan who came into my shop one day. He told me that a friend had suggested I could help. I took him to a pastor and asked him to baptize the man. When the pastor asked me if I'd start a home group to help support the young man, I said yes. And when, a year later, the young man himself asked if I would baptize him in church one Sunday, I said yes again.

My mom and dad joined us when we met every week. We prayed together, read the Bible a little, and talked about who Jesus was, why he died, and what it means to follow him. Not much more.

And when my mom asked if she could bring a friend along too, I said yes.

"She's a Muslim," Mom added.

The next week my mom's friend showed up. The Afghan man brought a few of his own friends too. They were Muslims. So there we all were, four Christians and six Muslims, all reading the Bible, talking about Jesus, and praying. Mom's friend wanted prayer for her son in Iran. He was a drug addict and very sick. We prayed. He got better, and the next week the mom gave her life to Jesus. Soon after that, the son did too. He said he met Jesus. In a mosque.

Soon we were not four Christians and six Muslims, but thirty people, some Christians, some Muslims, but all praying to Jesus. All expecting him to heal us. All learning to say "yes" to him.

We saw marriages restored, lives transformed, and so many refugees who were desperate for help turn to Jesus and give him their lives as a result. Whenever we prayed, I knew God would answer. And I knew that God had given me this job—to serve my people.

Soon we were too big to meet in my house, so we were invited to move to a church.

It seemed like God's work, so I just said yes.

―――

The work that God laid out for me didn't just wait until we started holding our church meetings. Even before then, more and more people were coming to the boutiques to see me and ask questions about God. I would invite people to the office out back and ask if they wanted me to pray. I never talked much about Islam, partly because of what had happened with Sarina, but mainly because

God never took me there. It was his Spirit that worked in people's lives, not my words or arguments.

I would pray in whichever of the two shops I was in each morning before I opened up. I would pray for the till, that the money might come in and be used for God's work. I prayed for the people who would visit, that God would be preparing the ground and show me what to say and how to pray. And I prayed for the power of God to be present, that even those who just walked in and looked at a few outfits would know something of God's love.

One morning my prayers took a little different turn.

"God, what do you want? Do you want me to build a business and have people come in and pray and meet you? Or do you want me in church, working with people there? If I'm staying I want to expand the business, to grow it all over the country. But if you want me in the church, take it all away from me so that I can be free."

Six hours later, my neighbor knocked on the shop door. He owned a Chinese restaurant and told me that he and his wife had been thinking how much they would like to make their premises bigger, and he asked if I would I sell them my shop. "We'll pay good money!"

I told my neighbor that I needed to think about it for two weeks. I knew God was at work, but did he have to move quite so fast? What was the plan? I prayed, but I heard nothing.

While I was waiting for an answer from God, Mina called from her university and said she was feeling sick, so I drove up to bring her home early for Christmas vacation. I had parked on campus, but never before had I seen the sign for the theology school. I told my sister to wait in the car while I went in to find out more.

I liked the feel of the place as I walked through the building and asked the receptionist if I could talk to someone about studying there. Ten minutes later a smart-looking lady came out, shook my hand, and suggested I come back next week to talk properly.

"I'm sorry, but I don't live here. I'll be back in Stockholm next week."

"No problem," the lady said. "I'll be down there next week. Let's meet."

Mina was skeptical when I got back in the car and told her what had happened. "Admissions officers don't visit out of school. I think you might have been confused there. You know your Swedish isn't all that good."

But the lady called as she promised the next week, and we sat and ate burgers as I told her my story. I left nothing out—not Asghar's violence, the reason why we left Iran, or the way that I had wrestled with the idea of becoming a pastor. I told her about the boutique and the man with the Chinese restaurant and the fact that, maybe, this was the time for me to finally say yes to God when, for so long, I had been saying no.

When I finished speaking she pulled a piece of paper out of her bag and slid it over to me. "If God chooses you, who am I to say no?"

It was an admissions form. I scanned it quickly and saw all the boxes in the academic qualifications that I would have to leave blank. I went to speak, but she interrupted me.

"If God chooses you, who am I to say no?"

———

Back home, it was Roksana's turn to be skeptical. "She can't really have the power to let you in the course like that, Mom. I think you must have gotten confused somewhere. Let me Google her name and see who she is anyway."

Roksana tapped a little on her computer, then fell silent. "Mom, she's not the admissions officer. She's the dean of the whole college."

That was that. It seemed God's prompting was clear. I sold the boutique to my neighbor and banked enough money to last the full four years of college. As my start date in August approached, I started getting nervous, and when the course itself began, I started feeling a whole lot worse. I was forty-four years old and over twice the age of most of the others in the room. They did everything so fast, with their phones and their laptops and their Swedish accents that I still had trouble following.

The hardest thing of all was the first time I had to get up in front of the class and tell my story. I had ten minutes to speak and years' worth of life to convey. I was in tears by the end of it and felt physically sick as I sat down. That night, I couldn't sleep.

I felt even worse the first time I was asked to preach and again share my testimony. My mom and dad were there this time. I knew that it would be the first time they had heard about Asghar's violence, about the truth behind our leaving Iran, about Turkey and the prison and everything else.

Again I felt sick as I finished and walked back to my seat. This time, I felt guilty as well. Should I have told them sooner? How would they cope?

I didn't see them until the end of the service. Both of them were silent, their faces drained in shock.

When we hugged, none of us ever wanted to let go.

SINCE THOSE FIRST COUPLE OF TIMES
when I finally broke my silence, I have told my story hundreds
of times, maybe thousands. I have told it to royalty and to refugees. I have shared it with people who know nothing of Islam and
people who know nothing of Jesus. I have spoken in hospitals and
churches, in front of television cameras and alone with just one
other person in my office sitting beneath the cross fixed to the wall.

One of those times came when I sat opposite a surly looking
seventeen-year-old. He had already told me that he would never
go to church and had only agreed to visit me out of respect to the
Swedish family who had adopted him.

"I respect Mohammed," he said. "There is nothing you can
say that could change my mind. But you, sister, would you like
to return to Islam? Allah can forgive you, and you can become a
Muslim again."

"No," I said, smiling a little but not so much as to give offense.
"I understand what you are saying. We both know about Islam,
so there's really no point in our talking about it, is there? But I
know about Jesus, and you don't. So why don't we start there?
Would you like to know him?"

"What could you tell me that would change anything about
what I believe?"

259

"Nothing. I can't show Jesus to you. Only Jesus can do that."
He thought for a moment.

"I don't understand."

"That's okay. We can pray together. Sometimes that helps."

"How?"

I pointed to the wall. "You see the cross there? Let's stand in front of it and pray."

As soon as we did, he started to cry.

"Jesus," I prayed. "I cannot show you to him. I cannot say anything about you to him. I want you to reveal yourself in his life. Please show him who you are."

He was trying so hard to hold in the tears. His face was reddening, and his body started to shake a little. Afghan men don't cry, especially not in front of women. But God was at work. The air was thick with the sense of it.

I prayed again. "It says in the Bible that every knee must bow before you and every tongue confess . . ."

He fell to his knees, unable to hold anything in for a second longer.

He wept for almost a whole hour, just like me in the home of the gray-haired neighbors, or Hussein at the meeting with thousands of people all around. I sat with him and thanked the Lord. I knew so little of his story, but I didn't need to. God was at work; that was enough.

When he was finished, I asked him what he had seen.

"I saw a place where the earth was rocky and hard. There was a little boy wearing white robes; then Jesus came in. He took the boy and hugged him. I was the boy."

"How do you feel now?"

"Like I know that Jesus was with me."

He went on to tell me a little about his life. He talked about the Taliban and how they had killed both his parents. By the time he was fifteen, he was an orphan and a refugee weighed down with so much pain and trauma as he tried to start a new life in Sweden.

"What do you want to say to your Swedish parents?"

"I want to become a Christian. How do I do it?"

I told him to lift his hands in prayer and repeat after me.

We all cried when I took him to his parents in the corridor outside. They asked me what I had said to him, and I told them the truth: "Nothing really. I just spoke a little about Jesus and asked him to help."

Sometimes the stories I hear from the refugees I work among remind me so clearly of my own life. So many of them have been wronged so greatly, and I talk a lot about Joseph's story in the Bible and how what was meant for harm, God can use for good. So many of them have so much to forgive. I often think about Asghar and how it took me years to forgive him. In the end, it was only with God's help that I could do it. Without forgiveness, those wounds can become toxic. Unless we fall on God for help, we can so easily become stuck.

Others are bound up by fear, just as I had been. They are terrified of losing their identity, of leaving Islam and their communities—as if leaving their homeland isn't hard enough. So I tell them about Ruth and how she was an alien in a foreign land, how she chose to follow Naomi's God instead of the one she had been brought up to believe in. And when she did, God used her. She had to choose God before he could use her.

Some are just so full of pain that as I listen I am taken back to the mountainside, to the pile of stones and the wolves' eyes that reflected in the firelight.

What do you say when confronted with pain, fear, and suffering like this? I say very little. I never talk about the differences between Islam and Christianity; for if life has taught me anything, it is that words can have power, but the Spirit of God is even greater still. If we want to see lives changed, the best thing we can do is step back and pray.

———

My life has changed so much, and not just on the outside. As far as my journey has taken me—so very far from my home and my old life in Iran—it is nothing compared to the transformation that God has gently nurtured within me. With his help I have left behind the feelings that once threatened to suffocate me.

For so many years, the only thing that kept me alive was the instinct to fight for my children. An anger burned within me, an instinct to protect them from all harm. God has even transformed that in wonderful ways. He has helped me to forgive, and he has also birthed within me a desire to fight for the people I meet who are desperate just like I was. And so I fight for something more than just my own survival or the survival of my children. I fight for those who need God. Even though I know that I am powerless, that God alone can rescue, I play whatever part God has for me to play.

I have learned to live without fear. After I became a Christian I wanted to keep life quiet and safe, to avoid any danger. So I tried to hide the truth about what Asghar had done to me. I was afraid that people would judge me, afraid that I would be a disappointment to them if I spoke of all the mess that my past contained. With God's help, I have let go of that. I am not afraid anymore. God is the one who keeps me safe. And he's the one who tells me: *Your story saves others. Tell it. Shout it from the rooftops. You have nothing to be ashamed of.*

———

One summer, as the news was full of almost daily coverage of refugees climbing on boats and hoping to make it to Greece, I was asked to pray with a man who had walked into the church.

Fiaz told me about the night that he, his wife, and two daughters stood on the shore in Turkey and watched the boats approach. The flashlights were weak and the waves crashing on the rocks were strong. He scooped up his little girls and called to his wife to follow.

The crowd was pressing on all sides. The water was cold, and the men who had taken all the money that Fiaz had left were shouting at everyone to hurry. He looked back, but it was too dark and there were too many people around for him to be able to see his wife.

Only when they had pushed away from the shore and the people froze still in terror as the waters came up over the sides did Fiaz discover that she had not made it on board. There were other boats, he told himself. She would have gotten on one of them.

When they landed he searched for her, checking frantically up and down the coast for any sign of her.

Nothing. He waited as long as he could, but his girls were cold, terrified, and needed to get somewhere warm. Eventually he had to leave the beach.

In the end, it took nine months for Fiaz to discover the truth. His wife had fallen down in the push to climb on board. She had drowned right there, just a few feet away from him. She was twenty-three.

"Only God can heal you," I said as Fiaz and I stood before the cross. "Open up your heart to him."

He let out a cry so raw, so loud, and so full of the deepest, darkest pain. It was the same cry as my own in the mountains. A rage against evil.

The next week Fiaz and his daughters moved in with a family from church. The journey ahead will be long for all of them. There will be no quick fixes and no simple solutions. But God will be with them, guiding them, leading and loving them. Every day he will be there for them to discover, reminding them of his love for them. He will call them back to him again and again and again. All they have to do is say yes and yes and yes.

I know this path they are on. I know the journey. It has taken so many years to reach this far, and I trust that however many years there are ahead, God will continue to guide and lead me. There will be pain ahead, and trouble and problems that I won't be able to fix on my own.

But in them all, I know God will be there, calling me to look to him. Inviting me to take the next step toward his open arms.

And I will say yes.

And yes.

And yes.

AFTERWORD

THANK YOU FOR SHARING THIS JOURNEY
with me. You may be wondering whatever happened to the three
constants in my story: Cherie, Daniel, and Roksana. I am happy
to say that God's protecting and guiding hand has been on all
three over the years.

Saying goodbye to Cherie when we started our new life in
Sweden was so painful. But we had no choice. We had to let her
go back to her father, Asghar. He did not treat her well, and eventually social services removed her and placed her in a sort of
youth housing until she was eighteen and able to look after herself. Today she is married, has a son, and still lives in Denmark.
Cherie broke all contact with Asghar after she left him, although
he tries to contact her on occasion. In 2008, by coincidence, she
and I got connected again. We had been searching for each other,
but both had changed our names. Today Cherie is once more a
part of our lives and we visit whenever we can.

Daniel is well. He studied political science and psychology
in college and is currently working in Stockholm where he lives
with his Rottweiler, Nato. After twenty-five years of prayer, Daniel

recently got baptized during our summer conference in 2017. I am so proud of him and grateful to God for this wonderful break-through. Listening to him read and talk about the Bible is one of the greatest joys in my life!

Roksana got her double bachelor in political science and international relations. She married in September 2016, lives in Stockholm, and is the chair of the Farsi church where I currently minister. Having worked as a press secretary for a political party, she is about to embark on a new career that God is leading her on.

As for me, I continue to follow God's call to serve former Muslims and to train churches on how to reach out and disciple them. It's been my privilege to be a part of the amazing work Jesus is doing, and I hope to keep walking alongside him in this way for years to come.

ACKNOWLEDGMENTS

I AM DEEPLY GRATEFUL TO MANY people for their help with this book. My children, Daniel and Roksana, and her husband, Thomas: you have been my inspiration to keep going. You have helped me to be bold and courageous, to follow God's calling and to share this story. My sister, Elina: your love and support gives me the strength to believe in myself. My parents: thank you for your guidance, love, and support. His majesty Carl XVI Gustaf and Queen Silvia of Sweden: thank you for inviting me to share my story and work with you. Anja Kontor: for the documentary that helped this story to first reach all over Sweden. Lars-Göran Carlsson and Tone Carlsson: for the opportunity to study at Johannelund Theological College and for teaching me about listening to and trusting God's word. Without that, my ministry wouldn't even be possible. Gordon Hickson: you were obedient to God and gave me the encouragement I needed at the perfect time. Craig Borlase: thank you for portraying something so heartbreaking in a way that shows God's unending love. Martin Raz and my agent Don Jacobson, Jessica

Wong, Heather Skelton, and the team at Thomas Nelson: you all believed in me and in this book. Thank you for taking a risk and seeing God's hand at work.

I thank God for each and every one of you.

ABOUT THE AUTHOR

ANNAHITA PARSAN IS AN ORDAINED minister in the Church of Sweden and leads two congregations, one of which ministers to the growing number of former Muslim refugees. She is a confident public speaker who has regularly shared her testimony with live audiences, journalists, and TV interviewers, even speaking one time at the invitation of the Queen of Sweden. She has worked pastorally with hundreds of former Muslims and regularly trains churches to reach out to Muslims and disciple them once they join the church.

CRAIG BORLASE (CRAIGBORLASE.COM) is a bestselling British author and collaborative writer of more than 40 books. He specializes in dramatic memoir driven by faith. His most recent books are *10,000 Reasons* with Matt Redman (David C. Cook), *Fleeing ISIS, Finding Jesus* with Charles Morris (David C. Cook) and *Finding Gobi* with Dion Leonard (Thomas Nelson).